# LATINOS IN THE UNITED STATES

## WHAT EVERYONE NEEDS TO KNOW®

**Also by Ilan Stavans**

**Fiction** *The Disappearance* * *The One-Handed Pianist and Other Stories*

**Nonfiction** *The Riddle of Cantinflas* * *Dictionary Days* * *On Borrowed Words* * *Spanglish* * *The Hispanic Condition* * *Art and Anger* * *Resurrecting Hebrew* * *A Critic's Journey* * *The Inveterate Dreamer* * *Octavio Paz: A Meditation* * *Imagining Columbus* * *Bandido* * *¡Lotería!* (with Teresa Villegas) * *José Vasconcelos: The Prophet of Race* * *Return to Centro Histórico* * *Singer's Typewriter and Mine* * *Gabriel García Márquez: The Early Years, 1929–1970* * *The United States of Mestizo* * *Reclaiming Travel* (with Joshua Ellison) * *Quixote: The Novel and the World* * *Borges, the Jew* * *I Love My Selfie* (with Adál)

**Conversations** *Knowledge and Censorship* (with Verónica Albin) * *What is la hispanidad?* (with Iván Jaksić) * *Ilan Stavans: Eight Conversations* (with Neal Sokol) * *With All Thine Heart* (with Mordecai Drache) * *Conversations with Ilan Stavans* * *Love and Language* (with Verónica Albin) * *¡Muy Pop!* (with Frederick Aldama) * *Thirteen Ways of Looking at Latino Art* (with Jorge J. E. Gracia) * *Laughing Matters* (with Frederick Aldama)

**Children's Book** *Golemito* (with Teresa Villegas)

**Anthologies** *The Norton Anthology of Latino Literature* * *Tropical Synagogues* * *The Oxford Book of Latin American Essays* * *The Schocken Book of Modern Sephardic Literature* * *Lengua Fresca* (with Harold Augenbraum) * *Wáchale!* * *The Scroll and the Cross* * *The Oxford Book of Jewish Stories* * *Mutual Impressions* * *Growing Up Latino* (with Harold Augenbraum) * *The FSG Books of Twentieth Century Latin American Poetry* * *Oy, Caramba!*

**Graphic Novels** *Latino USA* (with Lalo Alcaraz) * *Mr. Spic Goes to Washington* (with Roberto Weil) * *Once @ 9:53 am* (with Marcelo Brodsky) * *El Iluminado* (with Steve Sheinkin) * *A Most Imperfect Union* (with Lalo Alcaraz) * *Angelitos* (with Santiago Cohen)

**Translations** *Sentimental Songs*, by Felipe Alfau * *The Plain in Flames*, by Juan Rulfo (with Harold Augenbraum) * *The Underdogs*, by Mariano Azuela (with Anna More) * *Lazarillo de Tormes* * *El Little Príncipe*, by Antoine de Saint Exupéry

**Editions** *Cesar Vallejo: Spain, Take This Chalice from Me* * *The Poetry of Pablo Neruda* * *Encyclopedia Latina* (4 volumes) * *Pablo Neruda: I Explain a Few Things* * *The Collected Stories of Calvert Casey* * *Isaac Bashevis Singer: Collected Stories* (3 volumes) * *Cesar Chavez: An Organizer's Tale* * *Rubén Darío: Selected Writings* * *Pablo Neruda: All the Odes* * *Latin Music* (2 volumes)

**General** *The Essential Ilan Stavans*

# LATINOS IN THE UNITED STATES

## WHAT EVERYONE NEEDS TO KNOW®

### ILAN STAVANS

OXFORD
UNIVERSITY PRESS

# OXFORD
## UNIVERSITY PRESS

Oxford University Press is a department of the University of Oxford. It furthers the University's objective of excellence in research, scholarship, and education by publishing worldwide. Oxford is a registered trade mark of Oxford University Press in the UK and certain other countries.

"What Everyone Needs to Know" is a registered trademark of Oxford University Press.

Published in the United States of America by Oxford University Press
198 Madison Avenue, New York, NY 10016, United States of America.

Library of Congress Cataloging-in-Publication Data
Names: Stavans, Ilan, author.
Title: Latinos in the United States : what everyone needs to know / Ilan Stavans.
Description: New York, NY : Oxford University Press, 2018. |
Series: What everyone needs to know | Includes index.
Identifiers: LCCN 2017011697 | ISBN 9780190670184 (pbk. : alk. paper) |
ISBN 9780190670191 (hardcover : alk. paper) | ISBN 9780190670207 (Updf) |
ISBN 9780190670214 (Epub)
Subjects: LCSH: Hispanic Americans—History. | Hispanic Americans—Social life and customs. | Hispanic Americans—Social conditions.
Classification: LCC E184.S75 S763 2018 | DDC 973/.0468—dc23
LC record available at https://lccn.loc.gov/2017011697

1 3 5 7 9 8 6 4 2
Paberback printed by LSC Communications, United States of America
Hardback printed by Bridgeport National Bindery, Inc., United States of America

*To* mi cuate, *Frederick Luis Aldama*

All generalizations are false, including this one.

—Mark Twain

# CONTENTS

PREFACE: EL SUEÑO AMERICANO      XXIII

ACKNOWLEDGMENTS      XXIX

## 1 Nomenclature      1

*How did the term "Latino" come about?*      1

*When did "Hispanic" emerge?*      2

*Is the Caribbean Basin part of Latin America?*      4

*What are the most sizable groups in demographic terms?*      4

*Where do the majority of Latinos live?*      5

*Which states have the largest Latino concentrations?*      5

*The top five cities?*      5

*What is the gender ratio among Latinos?*      6

*What does it mean to be hyphenated?*      6

*Are Latinos different from other minorities?*      7

*What is* Latinidad*?*      8

*Is there a Latino aesthetic?*      8

*Do these aesthetics have a history?*      9

## 2  The Legacy of Colonization                                11

*Is the colonial period for the United States the same as for Latinos?*    *11*

*Is it possible to talk of Latinos as such in the colonial period?*    *12*

*Why talk about a common past?*    *12*

*Don't Latinos in the 21st century also have a common past?*    *12*

*Should Latinos then be understood as a by-product of colonialism?*    *13*

*How did Spanish missionaries engage with the indigenous population?*    *14*

*Who was Alvar Núñez Cabeza de Vaca?*    *16*

*What other types of "accounts" survive?*    *16*

*What was the function of the missions?*    *18*

*Why did the Spanish Empire collapse?*    *19*

*What kind of diplomatic relationship have Mexico and
the United States had over time?*    *20*

*Has the Rio Grande always served as the divide?*    *20*

*What kind of border existed before?*    *21*

*How did Latinos do under an independent Texas?*    *22*

*What happened at the Alamo?*    *22*

*What are the facts of the Battle of the Alamo?*    *23*

*How is the Alamo portrayed in art?*    *23*

*What was the cause of the Mexican-American War?*    *24*

*Were there other causes?*    *24*

*How did Mexico react to the annexation of Texas?*    *24*

*How did the war shape up?*    *25*

*Were Americans supportive of the effort?*    *25*

*What was the Treaty of Guadalupe Hidalgo about?*    *25*

*What was agreed?*    *26*

*What was the Gadsden Purchase about?*    *26*

How did Mexico react to the loss?                                           26

What role did Spain have in the Southwest after 1848?                       27

What was the Spanish-American War about?                                    27

What were the factors leading to that war?                                  28

What started it?                                                            29

Why was it called the Spanish-American War?                                29

How did the conflict evolve?                                               30

What about Hawaii?                                                         30

Who were the Rough Riders?                                                 30

What was the outcome of the war?                                          31

What happened with Cuba and Puerto Rico after Spain seceded
from the Caribbean Basin?                                                  31

Why was the Jones-Shafroth Act signed?                                    32

Did Latinos play a role in the two world wars?                            32

What were the circumstances of the Sleepy Lagoon Case?                    33

What role did the media play in the agitation?                            33

What were the Zoot Suit Riots about?                                      34

Does the understanding of history for Latinos change
after World War II?                                                       34

## 3 The Sleeping Giant                                                   36

Are Americans in general aware of the way Latinos as a minority are
a sum of parts?                                                           36

Do Latino loyalties follow party lines?                                   36

In general, how active are Latinos in politics?                           37

Do Latinos vote?                                                          38

What are the reasons Latinos don't register or vote?                      39

How does race affect participation?                                       40

And economic status?                                                              40

Who were the Latino political luminaries?                                          40

Are there pan-Latino leaders?                                                      41

What are the most prominent Latino political organizations?                       42

What are the traditional political loyalties of various national groups?          43

What kind of relationship has Cuba had with the United States?                    43

Who was Gerardo Machado?                                                          44

And Batista?                                                                      44

Who was Fidel Castro?                                                             44

How did Fidel Castro's revolution impact Latin America?                           45

And the United States?                                                            46

What role did Latinos play during the Civil Rights era?                           46

What were the tenets of the Chicano Movement?                                     47

Who was Cesar Chavez?                                                             47

What was his intellectual inspiration?                                            48

How did Chavez become a union leader?                                             48

What is Chicanismo?                                                               49

Where does the concept of la huelga come from?                                    49

How long did an average fast last?                                                50

Did religion play a role in Chavez's career?                                      50

What is Chavez's legacy?                                                          50

When did he die?                                                                  51

How should the concept of Aztlán be understood?                                   51

Where is Aztlán located?                                                          51

Is Aztlán seen as an attainable homeland?                                         52

What kinds of relationships were there between African Americans
and Chicanos during the Civil Rights era?                                         52

Who were the Puerto Rican Young Lords?                                            52

What role did Filipinos play in the Chicano Movement?                             53

Who was Reies López Tijerina?                                                     53

How about Rodolfo "Corky" González?                                              54

What was El plan espiritual de Aztlán?                                            55

What role did women play in the Chicano Movement?                           55

Is feminism a component of Chicanismo?                                      56

Who was Dolores Huerta?                                                     57

What is the legacy of the Chicano Movement?                                58

## 4  Yearning to Breathe Free                                             59

How is the word "immigration" defined?                                     59

What are the meanings of "exile" and "refugee"?                            59

Are all Latinos immigrants?                                                60

Is the term "illegal alien" derogatory?                                    60

What is the difference between an "immigrant" and a "migrant"?             60

Isn't the United States a country of immigrants?                           61

How have the waves of immigration changed over time?                       62

Has the United States ever encouraged immigration from the Americas?       62

Were there any laws regulating immigration before
the late 19th century?                                                     62

Have laws been implemented to exclude a singular ethnic group?             62

When did Mexicans become the largest group within the
Latino minority?                                                           63

Since they are de facto US citizens, why should Puerto Ricans be
considered immigrants?                                                     63

What caused the Puerto Rican migration?                                    63

Who were the jíbaros?                                                      64

What was the reason for their migration?                                   65

When did Puerto Ricans first settle in New York?                          65

What is the Loisaida?                                                      66

Why are Puerto Ricans perceived by other Latinos as unique?               66

Where is Vieques?                                                          66

Has there been another wave of Puerto Rican migration?                    67

Where does the word "Caribbean" come from?                                67

What kind of immigration took place after Fidel Castro's
1958–1959 revolution?                                                      67

How did the Cuban émigrés assimilate to the American way of life?  68

What kind of relationship does the exile community have with Havana?  68

What was Operation Peter Pan about?  69

What is the Mariel Boatlift?  69

What is a balsero?  70

What was the Elián Gonzáles affair about?  70

What about the Dominican Republic?  70

What caused the flight of immigrants from the Dominican Republic?  71

Where is the Dominican American community based?  71

Has immigration from Spanish-speaking countries always been incessant?  72

What is the apex of Central American immigration?  72

What kinds of wars?  73

What was the Iran-Contra Affair about?  74

How about immigration from South America to the United States?  74

Why has Colombia been a source of immigration?  75

And Venezuela: in what way have people from there been drawn to the United States?  75

Are Brazilians considered Latinos?  76

Where have Brazilians settled in the United States?  77

What brought along the Brazilian immigration?  77

What were living conditions like for Mexican immigrants in the United States during the 20th century?  78

What does bracero mean?  78

Was the program well received nationwide?  79

How many people were deported during Operation Wetback?  79

Have most undocumented immigrants come from Mexico?  79

Who are the DREAMers?  79

Did the DREAM Act pass?  80

Why deport undocumented immigrants to Mexico if half of them come from other countries?  80

Was Donald Trump the first US president to deport undocumented immigrants?  80

Was there legislation to counteract this massive movement? 80

Is deportation legal? 81

What about the mass protests of 2006? 81

Since when did the US-Mexico border become a nation unto its own? 82

When was the US Border Patrol formed? 83

Has the rationale for exclusion always used nationality? 83

What other acts followed? 83

Are anti-Trump protests connected to his views on deportation? 84

Is Trump anti-immigrants and anti-Latino? 84

Have Latino immigrants prospered in the United States? 84

What is the overall position of Latinos on immigration? 85

Is the issue of immigration linked to national security? 85

# 5 Family Secrets 86

Is la familia, the Latino family, closely knit? 86

In what way is that concept related to history? 86

Are there racial tensions among Latinos? 87

How did blacks come to the New World? 88

What is a mestizo? 88

How do Latinos perceive their indigenous past today? 89

In what sense are mestizaje and Afro-Latin identity different? 90

Will there ever be a postracial Latinidad? 90

Returning to la familia, what are its different roles? 90

What vision of manhood did the conquistadors bring along? 91

What is machismo? 91

What about marianismo? 91

What kind of support do mothers get from the community? 92

What about single-parent families? 92

Are divorces frequent? 92

How does the Latino community view abortion? 93

How do Latinos see childhood? 93

What are the challenges Latino children face?                               93

Is there child labor among Latinos?                                         94

What are the illnesses affecting children?                                  94

What about adolescent gangs?                                                94

Is ideology always defined?                                                 95

Do gangs have fixed internal structures?                                    95

Is gang participation among Latino youths higher than
among other minorities?                                                     96

What about incarceration?                                                   97

Is sexuality a forbidden topic among Latinos?                               97

What is the approach to abortion and birth control?                         98

How do Latinos understand homosexuality?                                    98

Who was Gloria Anzaldúa?                                                     99

Who is Richard Rodriguez?                                                    99

What are the challenges of the Latino LGBTQ community?                      100

Is marriage a strong institution?                                           100

What about the elderly?                                                      100

What is the Latino concept of death?                                        101

Have these concepts changed throughout time?                               101

What kinds of representations of death are available in
Latino culture?                                                             102

Are Latinos people of deep-seated faith?                                    102

What was the status of Catholicism in Spain in 1492?                        103

What kinds of religion existed in the Americas in pre-Columbian
civilization?                                                               103

What happened to the aboriginal religions in the colonial period?          104

When did Catholicism become the preeminent faith among Latinos
in the United States?                                                       104

What are the characteristics of Hispanic Catholicism in the Americas?      104

What Spanish versions of the Bible circulated in the New World?            104

Which is the most popular?                                                  105

What is Guadalupanismo?                                                     105

How did the Virgin of Guadalupe acquire her national stature?    106

What is her appeal?    106

What is the connection between the Virgin of Guadalupe and Latinos?    107

Did the United Farm Workers adopt her image?    107

Are there other Virgins?    107

What ethnic identity does she have?    108

What is her link to African traditions?    108

What is Santería?    108

Are ghosts a fixture in Latino life?    109

What about Protestantism?    109

Are there Jews in Latin America?    110

What percentage of Latinos in the United States is Jewish?    111

How about the number of Arabs?    111

When was the Qur'an translated into Spanish and available in
the United States?    112

How many Latino Jews are there?    112

What role do indigenous practices play among Latinos?    113

What about Afro-Caribbean beliefs?    113

Are younger Latinos less religious?    113

# 6 Fusión Latina    114

What is fusión latina?    114

Is music the most vibrant of artistic manifestations among Latinos?    115

What kind of history does Latin music have in the United States?    115

Do different national groups have different musical forms?    115

And classical music?    116

What different instruments are used?    116

What is a corrido?    117

Does the tradition continue?    117

And narcocorridos?    118

What about tejano and conjunto music?                                    118

Who was Selena?                                                          118

What are plenas?                                                         119

Is there a difference between merengue and bachata in the
Caribbean and in the United States?                                     119

What kind of influence has Brazil exerted in Latino music?              119

What different types of salsa are there?                                119

Who was Celia Cruz?                                                      120

What is Latino hip-hop?                                                  120

Why is reggaetón so popular?                                            121

Who are the leaders of Latin Jazz?                                      121

How about dance?                                                        121

How about dance clubs?                                                  122

Is pictorial art equally important?                                     122

How about muralism?                                                     123

And street art?                                                         123

And comic strips?                                                       124

Is there a particular type of Latino graffiti?                          124

What are Lowriders?                                                     125

What about Latino theater?                                              125

Who was Luis Valdez?                                                    126

What are Valdez's most famous plays?                                    126

How about Lin-Manuel Miranda?                                           127

What about TV?                                                          127

Since when have Latinos been active in American television?             127

What is a telenovela?                                                   128

Who is Jorge Ramos?                                                     128

What about variety shows on TV?                                         129

Is there a Latino cinema?                                               129

What about Latino actors in Hollywood?                                  130

And radio?                                                             130

Who was Rubén Salazar?                                    131

How did Salazar die?                                      132

What are the varieties of Latino folklore?               133

Who are the most important ethnographers?                133

Is there a Latino literary tradition?                    134

Who are the founding figures of fiction?                 135

Who was Felipe Alfau?                                     135

What are the Latino literary classics?                   136

What makes Junot Díaz a trailblazer?                     136

What about poetry?                                        137

Who are their successors?                                137

How about memoirs?                                       138

Who was Oscar "Zeta" Acosta?                             138

What are the favorite genres?                            139

How has literature represented the Cuban exile?          140

When did the field of Latino Studies emerge?             140

What about the Spanish-language book industry?           141

Did the Spanish-language publishing industry change with the
Chicano Movement?                                        142

Are there more small presses?                            142

Which are the most censored books by Latino authors in the
United States in the 21st century?                       143

Do Latinos excel at sports?                              143

What kinds of sports are popular in Latin America?       144

Were there pre-Columbian sports?                         145

Is soccer relevant to Latinos in the United States?      146

How are sports covered in Spanish-language media?        147

Since when are Latinos visible in the Major Leagues?     147

When did Latinos enter the Major Leagues?                148

What other sports are popular?                           148

Is tennis played by everyone?                            148

And wrestling?                                                              149

What about bullfighting?                                                    149

How about other types of games?                                            150


# 7  Words and Power                                                        **151**

Are Latinos contemporaries of the rest of America?                         151

What are the characteristics that make a Latino teacher?                   151

Is the American classroom a welcoming place for Latinos?                   152

What are the foremost challenges?                                          153

Do Latinos learn in a different way?                                       153

Should there be preferential treatment for these minorities?              153

How does bilingualism define the education of Latinos?                     154

Was Bilingual Education successful?                                        155

Are there similar programs for other minorities?                          155

Why are Latinos underrepresented in higher education?                      156

Is activism a common path for Latino students in higher education?         156

Are there teachers who have become role models?                           156

Does the word have power?                                                  157

Moving on to the topic of words, is there such a thing
as purity in language?                                                     158

Does language have larger political implications?                          158

How many people speak Spanish in the United States?                        158

Since when has Spanish been present in the United States?                  159

Is there one Spanish in Latin America or are there many?                   160

Is language a prism whereby to understand the conquest?                    161

How did Spanish replace the aboriginal tongues in the region?             161

What happened with Spanish during the colonial period?                     162

What is the English-Only Movement?                                         162

What is English-First?                                                     163

Is English the official language of the United States?                     163

Have all immigrant groups had bilingual education?                         164

*What is Spanglish?* 164

*When does automatic translation occur?* 165

*What about the coining of Spanglishisms?* 165

*Is there only one Spanglish in the United States?* 165

*What is the use of Spanglish in commerce and the media?* 166

*Is its use prevalent in business?* 167

*And in politics?* 167

*Are the translations of literary classics into Spanglish available?* 168

*Is there an equivalent of the Royal Academy of the Spanish
Language in Spanglish?* 170

**EPILOGUE: 100 ARTIFACTS** 171

**AFTERWORD: WE ARE ALL DREAMERS** 177

**FURTHER READING** 181

**INDEX** 185

# PREFACE: EL SUEÑO AMERICANO

Walt Whitman once said that the genius of America "is not best or most in its executives or legislatures, nor in its ambassadors or authors or colleges, or churches, or parlors, nor even in its newspapers or inventors, but always most in the common people." Indeed, because the common people are permanently on the move, America itself exists in a state of becoming—that is, it is never static, it is constantly changing.

That change is tangible in its social mobility. One might be born at the bottom of the economic scale but, unlike what happens in other parts of the world, it doesn't mean that person remains there forever. Just as money at the top moves around, incentives at the bottom serve as an engine of progress.

Progress—the idea of it!—gives the nation its traction. That progress is alluring to others elsewhere in the planet who dream of a better life. They have been coming, those "common people," as immigrants to these shores to partake in the dream of progress.

Yet the question emerges: is mobility attainable to all? Does el Sueño Americano, the American Dream, still serve as a motivator?

That question is at the heart of the age of Donald Trump. To understand its impact, it is important to keep in mind that a dramatic shift, in terms of immigration, took place in the second half of the 20th century. Until then and with the exception of the slave trade, the majority of newcomers to these shores had as their point of departure the Old World, such as places like Ireland, Italy, France, Germany, Scandinavia, Greece, and Poland. In racial terms, people were for the most part Caucasians. The response to their arrival was based on class and costumes: they were discriminated against because they were poor and illiterate, and they brought with them different cultural attitudes. After World War II, an entirely different wave of immigrants, with different skin colors, entered the country: people from places like Korea and China, India and Pakistan, Vietnam and Cambodia, Nigeria and Senegal, Lebanon and Iran, the Francophone and Spanish-speaking Caribbean, and everywhere in Latin America.

As a result, America has been undergoing a redefinition of its national identity, one in which multiculturalism plays a central role. Metropolises like Los Angeles, San Antonio, Houston, Miami, and New York are no longer white bastions but rainbow cities defined by ethnic differences. And the social change has taken place, albeit at a slower speed, in rural areas, where small communities have experienced the demographic growth of ethnic minorities.

At the same time, a large portion of the white population, predominantly in these rural areas, feels left behind. Its jobs have disappeared as trade agreements have been established between the United States and its North American neighbors, Canada and Mexico, and between the United States and Europe. Likewise, the enormous growth of the Chinese economy has redesigned the corporate map. More goods are needed at cheaper prices and it is more financially feasible to produce them in developing countries.

The animosity of this largely rural, non-college-educated class is often targeted toward immigrants in general. And because of illegal immigration, among other factors, Latinos frequently get the brunt of it. Not all in equal measure, though. In the Trump age, Mexicans in particular, constituting almost two-thirds of the total Hispanic population, are demonized.

This demonization is played out through stereotypes: criminals, rapists, drug dealers, and so on. Yet Latinos aren't only the fastest-growing group in America; they are also the biggest. In the past several decades, the United States has the second largest concentration of Spanish-speaking people in the world after Mexico. This means that there are more Latinos in America than Colombians in Colombia or Argentineans in Argentina.

They are a singular group in that while a substantial number of Mexicans in the United States are immigrants, others were in these lands before the War of Independence. Their entrance to the middle class is steady, although it hasn't occurred at the same speed than it has for some other immigrant groups.

From *América* to America, their transculturation (sociologists still call it "assimilation") is a development whereby their customs get acclimated to the new environment. In the past, that development was seen as a renunciation: the newcomer renounced his or her culture in order to be like everyone else in a new country. That, basically, was the assumption behind the theory of the "melting pot": different ancestries melted to the point of becoming American. The current approach replaces the concept of the melting pot with that of a mosaic. In the age of multiculturalism, America no longer forces immigrants to leave behind the baggage they arrived with; instead, society is perceived as a parade of possibilities unified by a common set of symbols (a flag, an anthem, a connection to place) and motifs (a shared sense of history, the belief in individual achievement, and the moral commitment to help those in need).

Again, under the Trump administration this change from melting pot to mosaic is perceived as a threat. The nation's core values, it is argued, are no longer embraced with equal fervor as before.

Be that as it may, it is often said that in the 21st century the United States is being *Hispanized*. That is, Latinos are increasingly redefining the social mosaic through cuisine, music, sports, and political representation. A similar trend is taking place south of the Rio Grande, where American culture has been impregnating every aspect of life since the second half of the 20th century. When these two transformations are considered together, it is clear that an erasing of differences is under way.

This is ironic because as Latin America struggles to stabilize itself economically and politically, the US-Mexico border has been turned into a veritable wound—an abyss, not only physical but metaphorical, separating two distinct worldviews.

How quickly Latinos will become an essential component of the nation might be measured by the incorporation of their history into textbooks. Their plight, explored with depth and complexity, is still absent, although some states have made substantial advances on this front. After all, Latinos aren't a recent arrival. Their history in the United States goes back hundreds of years. And they have played a fundamental role at every turn.

Might a time come soon when their plight will be on display in a museum on the Washington Mall, part of the Smithsonian, and next to others memorializing the black experience, the Holocaust, and the war in Vietnam?

Latinos' contested presence in America today doesn't allow for such possibility in the foreseeable future. For the time being, the effort appears to be more basic: debunking stereotypes, which are nothing but generalizations.

This book uses the Q&A as its structure, which lends itself to jazzy improvisation. The urge to go deeper on countless themes is constantly being tested against the need to keep a straight argument, to offer a picture of the forest through the trees without turning any one of the trees into a forest unto itself. I have organized the topics into eight chapters that rotate around rather general themes, such as politics, nationality, economics, religion, education, entertainment, and language. Instead of isolating any of these, I build a web that connects them, going from the macro to the micro.

Early on in the book, I present Latino history as "a common past." By this I mean an undifferentiated, combined history that spans from the colonial period (1492–1810) to World War II (1939–1945), a period in which national groups were conflated into a single whole. Of course, this is exactly what happened from the Civil Rights era (1954–1968) onward, although for different reasons. Whereas in the earlier, formative years national identities weren't seen by Latinos and others as unifying categories, at the end of the 20th century the homogenization of Latinos was built precisely on the premise of their heterogeneity.

*Mestizaje*—or mixing, not only in racial terms—is what defines Latinos as a minority. And such intermixing, manifested in myriad ways, is the essential contribution of Latinos to the United States. If W. E. B. DuBois argued that the 20th century was about the color line, my intuition (and there is plenty of evidence already) is that the 21st century will be about miscegenation.

A few caveats: I use the word "America" to refer to a country as well as to the entire continent, although I make sure the distinction is never unclear; I refer to the natives of the Americas as Indians, aboriginal, and indigenous people depending on the context; and while I prefer the term "Latino" (but not, as I make clear in due time, "Latin@"), I use it almost interchangeably with "Hispanic," even though the latter is most often applied to people living in the Hispanic world as a whole.

# ACKNOWLEDGMENTS

The original idea began a decade ago, with an invitation by Donna Sanzone of Collins Publisher, in partnership with John Fehr and Pilar O'Leary at the Smithsonian in Washington, D.C., to reflect on Latino identity, politics, and culture. They engaged Jennifer Acker, who did an extensive month-long Q&A with me on the topic. The outcome was *Collins Q&A: Latino History and Culture* (2007).

By definition, a work of this type is always subject to additions and subtractions. Recently, the speed of affairs in the United States has resulted, among other things, in a reassessment of the role that Latinos play. As Barack Obama's last year in office came to a close and Donald Trump was elected president, an altogether different age was heralded in. It was then when I received another invitation, this one from Marcela Maxfield of Oxford University Press, to return to the topic in the same format, bringing it up to date.

In that spirit, I reworked the material thoroughly. The current volume broadens the picture, making it more nuanced in parts and reformulating its basic premises in others. I have presented the material in such a way as to defy disciplines. After all, knowledge is only compartmentalized by scholars. In the actual world, it is free and boundless and continuous.

Angela Chnapko, editor extraordinaire, inherited the project from Maxfield. Her sharp eye read the manuscript with meticulous attention, suggesting valuable improvements. Such was her acumen that at various points during the editorial process I felt as if I were having a Q&A with her. Her assistant, Alexcee Bechthold, helped navigate the editorial process. Shalini Balakrishnan, in Chennai, India, was in charge of production. Christine Dahlin did the copyediting and Neal Sokol compiled the index.

Gracias to all of them for making these reflections possible.

# LATINOS IN THE UNITED STATES

## WHAT EVERYONE NEEDS TO KNOW®

# 1

# NOMENCLATURE

## *How did the term "Latino" come about?*

An attempt at understanding the essential role Latinos play in America needs to start with a basic etymological discussion. The term "Latino" came about in the late 20th century to describe the rich, heterogeneous minority made up of people with roots in different parts of what once was the Spanish Empire, which spread from the island of Puerto Rico to the archipelago of the Philippines, from the northern Sonora desert in Mexico to the frigid Argentina Pampas. Since the colonial period—in fact, since before the anchoring of the *Mayflower* in Provincetown Harbor, Cape Cod—there were Hispanic bastions, such as missions, settlements, and encampments in Florida and different parts of what are today the southwestern states of Arizona, New Mexico, Texas, and California. In the middle of the 19th century, after the signing of the Treaty of Guadalupe Hidalgo and the Gadsden Purchase, the Spanish-speaking population in these areas became part of the United States. They were *Mexicanos, Tejanos,* and *californios.*

Meanwhile, some Cubans began establishing business endeavors in Key West. Then, in the early days of the 20th century, as a result of the Jones-Shafroth Act, another national group fell under the American expansionist spell: Puerto Ricans. And as the waves of history changed, other south-of-the-border dwellers made their way to various geographical points, from Missouri to Oregon, from New York to Rhode Island. There were a variety of ways to refer to them, including—and depending on their background—*braceros* and *jíbaros*. There were also some more derogatory appellations, such as "spics" and "greasers."

Each of these national groups retains its own rubrics: at various times, Mexican Americans have also been called Chicanos, People of Aztlán, and Mex-Americans; Puerto Ricans in New York are known as Nuyorricans; and so on. As the various national groups found each other and political alliances were established, more cohesive categories were sought: *hispano* and Spanish were popular in the 1960s. It was during the Nixon administration that the term "Hispanic" was first used in government documents, including in Census questionnaires. However, the term carried a heavy historical baggage, signaling the relevance Spain played in the colonial effort. (Hispania was the name for Spain during the Roman Empire.) In 1992, the quincentennial of Christopher Columbus's landing in the Bahamas generated much soul-searching. People felt some distance from that historical episode needed to be established. A different term— "Latino"—was preferred.

Its etymology too might be confusing. The word "Latino" is traceable to Hellenistic civilization, in particular to the Roman code of law. In the 19th century, as the republican spirit for independence sped throughout the Americas, emerging nations embraced the code in their judicial system. After the revolutionary figure Simón Bolívar, known as El Libertador, fought to create a consortium of republics in South America, a number of Chilean exiles in Paris, looking to find commonalities between the different nations, came up with *l'Amerique latine*.

### When did "Hispanic" emerge?

Language exists in a state of constant change. Words used nowadays are out of fashion tomorrow and meaning is modified according to the need of users. "Latino" is *la palabra del día*, the word of the day. Its currency denotes an ideological intention, for it attempts to understand the minority—which, according to the U.S. Census Bureau will, by the year 2025, constitute one fourth of the overall population of the United States—not as a sum of disconnected national groups but as a sum of parts. That is, there might not be a "real" Latino anywhere because people are more particular in their identity: Nicaraguan Americans, Costa Rican Americans, and Venezuelan Americans, among others. Nonetheless, this fragmentation might work at the individual level but not when it comes to politics, education, and the media. For better or worse, the main US parties, Republican and Democratic, approach Latinos as a unified entity, and so do school administrators, job agencies, school administrators, and radio and TV networks.

For purposes of this discussion, and in order to minimize confusion, the term "Hispanic" is used to refer to a person anywhere in the so-called *civilización hispánica*, from the Iberian Peninsula to the Caribbean Basin and throughout the Spanish-speaking Americas. People from different parts are called by their national background: Panamanians, Uruguayans, Chileans, and others. The term "Caribbean" is used for someone living in Cuba, Puerto Rico, the Dominican Republic, Jamaica, Haiti, or the Bahamas. "Latin American" denotes someone from the area on the southern side of the US-Mexico border to Tierra del Fuego, the continent's tip near Antarctica. For a Mexican in the United States, either as a result of immigration or by birth, the term used is "Mexican-American." The same goes for other national groups. And "Latino" is the rubric used for the Hispanic people in the United States, either by birth or as a result of immigration.

It is important to emphasize that, contrary to what is commonly assumed, not every Latino speaks Spanish. Equally important is the fact that this minority cannot be defined through categories like race, class, and religion. In racial terms, Latinos come in all shapes and forms: black, mestizo,

Asian, white, and there are middle-class Latinos as well as poor and rich Latinos and Latinos within every economic level in between. Plus the minority is made of people embracing Catholicism, Protestantism, Judaism, Islam, and Buddhism, among other affiliations.

### Is the Caribbean Basin part of Latin America?

The Caribbean Basin is an archipelago of divergent futures. Aside from indigenous and creole languages, those living there speak Spanish, English, and French. The Spanish-speaking portion of the basin (Cuba, Puerto Rico, Dominican Republic) is considered part of Latin America.

Puerto Rico, settled by Spanish conquistadors and missionaries, became a satellite of the United States during the Spanish-American War and was incorporated into a commonwealth in 1917. The Dominican Republic has remained independent but has experienced a military dictatorship and financial ruin. And Fidel Castro, a bearded rebel who plotted to overtake the Cuban government in 1958 from his headquarters in Sierra Maestra, turned Cuba into a Marxist-Leninist safe heaven while redefining the hemisphere's political board. The exile of millions of people from the island created another Cuba, *la Cuba de afuera*, the outside Cuba. These three diasporas are an essential component of the Latino minority in the mainland.

### What are the most sizable groups in demographic terms?

Mexicans have always been the largest group within the Hispanic minority in the United States. For a long time their geographic base was in the Southwest, particularly California, Texas, New Mexico, Colorado, and Arizona. Since the 1970s, labor opportunities have mobilized this group. By the 21st century, roughly seven out of ten Latinos were of Mexican background and all major cities in the United States had a Mexican presence. In 2015, almost 18% of the total US population, close to 60 million, was Latino.

Although a significantly smaller portion of the US population, other large groups are from the Caribbean: Puerto Ricans, Cubans, and Dominicans. The number of Central Americans—Salvadorans, Nicaraguans, Guatemalans, and Hondurans—is also ample.

It is important to point out that whereas in 1960 almost the entire Hispanic minority in the United States was composed of foreign-born Latinos, by 2015 only two out of every five Latinos came from outside the United States.

### Where do the majority of Latinos live?

Predominantly in the West and in the South. A vast number of Latinos live in urban centers, although small rural communities abound in Oregon, Utah, Arizona, Colorado, and New Mexico. Approximately six out of every ten Latinos is Mexican American. Then come Puerto Ricans, Cubans, and a large category defined as "other," which is subdivided into Dominican Americans, Central Americans, and South Americans.

### Which states have the largest Latino concentrations?

In descending order, Texas, California, New Mexico, Arizona, and Nevada. This sequence, of course, changes along with demographic density

### The top five cities?

In 2016, the five cities with the largest Latino concentrations were Hialeah, Florida (94.7% are Latinos); Laredo, Texas (94.1%); Brownsville, Texas (92.5%); McAllen, Texas (81.3%); and El Paso, Texas (80%). Of course, in terms of cities that have the largest total number of Latinos, the list is different: New York City (2.27 million are Latinos); Los Angeles

(1.8 million); Houston, Texas (908,000); San Antonio, Texas (807,000); followed by Chicago (774,000).

### What is the gender ratio among Latinos?

Roughly six out of every ten Latinos are male, and four are female. The unbalance is the result of immigration patterns, and immigration is a decisive factor in the making of the Latino minority. The perilousness of the journey attracts more men than women.

### What does it mean to be hyphenated?

Merriam-Webster defines a hyphen as "a punctuation mark used especially to divide or to compound words, word elements, or numbers." In the 1980s, a new nomenclature emerged among sociologists to refer to minorities: Italian Americans, African Americans, Jewish Americans, Irish Americans, and so on. Prior to this the usage was a single pronoun: Italians, Blacks, Jews, Irish, and so on. This phenomenon responded to a different approach to identity, individual and collective, in the United States. Up until then, immigrants in America were expected to leave behind, through the slow process of assimilation, their cultural ancestry, in favor of full integration. That was the meaning of the metaphor "melting pot," a term coined by the British-Jewish author Israel Zangwill in a 1908 play of the same name.

As mentioned before, in time "melting pot" was deemed by specialists to be too harsh a term. Why couldn't immigrants retain aspects of their backgrounds while also embracing American mores? Other metaphors have come to the rescue, including "salad bowl," "kaleidoscope," and "mosaic." The hyphen as a qualifier of American identity is essential among them: Latino Americans are at once Latino and Americans. Yet what distinguishes this hyphenated concoction is that identity is often found in the hyphen itself, that is, neither on one side nor the other but in the middle. The hyphen is thus seen as a bridge, a link, a connector.

### Are Latinos different from other minorities?

Unquestionably, they are different. That difference is the result of a variety of factors. Geography is one. Whereas other minorities come to the United States from far away, the place called home for Latinos is often rather close, as in the case of Mexico, Cuba, Puerto Rico, and the Dominican Republic. Another distinguishing factor is that a generous portion of Latinos were in this country—in Florida and the Southwest, among other places—even before 1776, when the United States declared its independence. That is, their existence in America precedes America itself.

Then there is the fact that whereas other immigrant groups in the second half of the 19th century and the early decades of the 20th, for instance, Irish Americans, Italian Americans, Jewish Americans, and so on, came as immigrants from particular socioeconomic backgrounds, Latinos arriving to America are from upper, middle, and lower classes. And more than most other immigrant groups, they are from a variety of racial heritages: mestizo, Caucasian, black, indigenous, and so forth.

Finally, a crucial factor differentiating Latinos from other minorities is reflected in the incessant immigration trends. Other minorities, such as Jewish Americans, came, for the most part, at a specific time—around 1880 in the case of immigrants from Eastern Europe (Poland, Russia, Ukraine, and Belarus), and the immigration wave concluded by 1930. But the waves among Latinos cannot be pinned to a particular year. Immigration from the Spanish-speaking world to the United States has been a constant since the mid-19th century, when the Treaty of Guadalupe Hidalgo of 1846 concluded the Mexican-American War.

This last factor is decisive in understanding why assimilation for Latinos at times feels protracted. Just as Nicaraguans ceased coming to America, Dominicans began arriving. And when the number of Dominicans decreased, large waves came from Venezuela. Among other things, the incessant onslaught helps explain the endurance of Spanish—in contaminated form—as a valuable language of communication in the United States today.

### What is Latinidad?

*Latinidad* is a style—in Spanish, *"una manera de ser, de pensar, de soñar,"* a way of being, thinking, and dreaming—that describes the culture of Latinos in the United States without reducing that culture to a single attribute. It is a way of enjoying life that comes not from one national background in the Hispanic minority but from the interaction of all of them in the American ecosystem. "Hispanidad" is a larger category, encompassing those from Spain, Latin America, the Spanish-speaking Caribbean, and Latinos in the United States.

Personally, though at times I use the term "Latino" and "Hispanic" interchangeably, I prefer the former. Since it comes from the Spanish and ends in a vowel, it isn't gender-neutral. ("Hispanic," by contrast, ends with a consonant.) In the past decade, there has been a movement inside academia to make "Latino" inclusive, transforming it to "Latina/o" or "Latin@."

### Is there a Latino aesthetic?

An aesthetic should be understood as a cultural approach to sensuous perceptions. Or, better, as a unified sense of taste shared by people from the same geographical, cultural, political, and artistic realm.

The Hispanic world is the result of a process of syncretism. The cultures of the Iberian Peninsula and the Americas fused into an amalgamation that borrowed from each side. That fusion has never been fixed. It remains ongoing, adapting to new circumstances. In Mexico and Central America, it has given place to mestizo aesthetics, whereas in Cuba, Puerto Rico, and the Dominican Republic it has produced an Afro-Caribbean sense of taste.

Latinos in the United States have inherited this fusion. In turn, they have adapted it to their context, giving place to a distinct sensibility, part Hispanic, part Anglo. That sensibility is often contained in the concept of Spanglish.

Such is the heterogeneity of the minority that the aesthetics vary, depending on class, race, nation, generation, language, and geography. A working-class Chicano in San Antonio, while sympathizing with the Latino aesthetic, approaches it individually through *rascuachismo*, a term denoting a sense of empowerment about pop Chicano culture. For him, the Virgin of Guadalupe and popular comedians like Cantinflas or Tin Tan might be icons. A middle-class Cuban-American in Miami will embrace a different artistic constellation: Gloria Estefan and Santería. The approach in this case is *tropicalismo*, inspired by a Brazilian artistic movement around Oswald de Andrade's 1928 artistic manifesto "Anthropophagy."

### Do these aesthetics have a history?

In major urban centers Latinos congregate according to national background. There are the Mexican American neighborhoods of La Villita and Pilsen in Chicago, Miami-Dade and Broward in Miami, and Jackson Heights in New York. They share common elements: language, a passion for music and sports, and a flavorful cuisine. But a combined aesthetic sensibility has yet to be articulated in a convincing fashion. When it does, it shall be clear that its roots are in the *santos* and *devotos* of colonial art in the Southwest and that it owes much to the south-of-the-border aesthetic movements like *Modernismo* and *Indigenismo*. The first came about in 1885 and had as its central promoter the Nicaraguan poet Rubén Darío. Its objective was for Latin American artists and thinkers to break away from their dependency to Spain. The second, an afterthought of the interpretations of José Enrique Rodó's groundbreaking book *Ariel* (1900), asks for a return to indigenous culture as a source of hemispheric identity.

The aesthetic of Spanglish is about double consciousness. It embraces cross-cultural and polyglot culture. It rejects purity as a form of originality and stresses the value of borrowings. It also elevates kitsch—derivative art produced for the consumption of the masses—as a legitimate form of expression.

# 2

# THE LEGACY
# OF COLONIZATION

## Is the colonial period for the United States the same as for Latinos?

No, it isn't. Historically, the colonial period in the United States is the time between the arrival of the English Separatists on the *Mayflower* in 1620 and the subsequent foundation of colonies like the one in Plymouth between 1620 and 1691. This period lasted until the Revolutionary War of 1776, when the nation ceased to be a colony of England. In the Hispanic world, and thus for Latinos in the United States, the colonial period lasted from 1492, with the arrival of Columbus in Hispaniola, until 1810, when Mexico, then called New Spain, became the first colony in the Spanish-speaking Americas to fight for its independence. Thus, the Latino colonial period was longer.

For Latinos in what is today the United States (Florida, California, Texas, and other parts of the Southwest), the colonial period is defined not by a runaway separatist sect but by the period during which the Spanish Empire controlled its colonies across the Atlantic.

By the way, just as the colonial period for Latinos is different from that of the United States as a whole, so is their overall history. Needless to say, there are numerous intersections between the two. Yet Latino history is unique and needs to be understood as such. Within that history, the colonial period remains one of the least studied.

### Is it possible to talk of Latinos as such in the colonial period?

Not quite. The formation of a cohesive Hispanic identity didn't take place until much later. Starting with the encounter between European and indigenous populations, and through a process of miscegenation known as *mestizaje*, Latin America evolved over several centuries. It became a region with its own clearly defined collective identity, with elements from aboriginal cultures, Spain and Portugal, Africa through the slave trade, and immigrants from Europe, Asia, and the Far East. *Latinidad*, as a tangible cultural term, emerges only at the end of the 20th century.

### Why talk about a common past?

The concept of "a common past" results from approaching what later would become Latino culture as an entity with roots in the colonial period. There were Catholic missions founded by proselytizing in Florida, New Mexico, Texas, and California. Missionaries taught the indigenous population in the areas the Spanish language, and, through it, the catechism as understood by Spain's Catholic Church. People then were not yet Cuban, Mexican, Puerto Rican, and so on. Thus, although the colonial era is approached as a time before national identities became qualifiers to understand specific groups, the foundations of Spanish civilization were ingrained in the new culture.

### Don't Latinos in the 21st century also have a common past?

They certainly do, although that commonality—that is, Latinos as a unified whole, and not as, for example, Mexican Americans, Cuban Americans, or Dominican Americans—is based on the idea that these distinct national groups have, nevertheless, elements in common: Spanish as a language, a shared sense of history, a religious heritage, and so forth.

### Should Latinos then be understood as a by-product of colonialism?

The departure from the port of Palos in Spain of Christopher Columbus's three caravels, the *Niña*, the *Pinta*, and the *Santa María*, took place on August 3, 1492. After a near mutiny of the fleet, the ships arrived in the Bahamas on October 12. The date is celebrated in the United States as Columbus Day and in the Spanish-speaking world as *Día de la Raza*. The journey came at a time when Spain was expanding its colonial borders and its economy was stagnant. Muslims and Jews were expelled from the Iberian Peninsula or forced to convert. Catholicism was turned into the nation's centralizing religion in *La Reconquista*, as the effort to reconquer Spain from the "infidels" came to be known. In what is today Florida, Louisiana, New Mexico, Arizona, Utah, Colorado, Utah, California, and Oregon, a series of Spanish explorers and missionaries like Alvar Núñez Cabeza de Vaca, Juan de Oñate, Juan de Castellanos, Father Eusebio Kino, and Fray Marcos de Niza first surveyed the land, then colonized it, with the Bible as their code of conduct. They imposed a different language and worldview on the population in the region.

Even though strictly speaking there are no more colonies today, colonialism as a state of mind exerts an enormous impact on us. The imperial endeavor of European nations in Asia, Africa, and the Americas left behind a series of structurally marked societies whose dependency on foreign support (financial, religious, medical, pedagogical, and technological) lingers without end. As a result, a colonial mentality shapes the way the world is perceived. Not unless and until the legacy of the colonial period is understood in full will a more enlightened approach to culture in general be available. That sense of dependency defines Latinos too.

*How did Spanish missionaries engage
with the indigenous population?*

While Latinos have been an essential component of the American mosaic, their role in the nation's history hasn't been fully appreciated. If, on the one hand, the starting point of this history is the series of events that defined the birth of the republic in 1776, it is important to emphasize that, while the Hispanic population in the Northeast at the time was minuscule, it was already quite diversified on the opposite coast. If, on the other hand, we look to a history not about the struggle for American independence by figures like George Washington, Thomas Jefferson, and John Adams, but about the civilization encountered and transformed by the European explorers who crossed the Atlantic, then the search for historical origins reaches back to the early decades of the 16th century. The debate over when Latino history begins polarizes scholars: are the Latino roots in the colonial period too tenous? Are the Iberian soldiers and missionaries true ancestors of say the Cuban Americans and Chilean Americans of today? Does it start, instead, as part of Mexican history, recognizing that before the current Latino population of the Southwest became American it was part of the country known in the colonial period as New Spain? The approach endorsed by most historians, however, uses geography as its rationale. The territories of Utah, Nevada, and Colorado changed hands frequently.

Nevada might be used as an example. It was annexed as part of New Spain, part of what was known as the Commandancy General of the Provincias Internas. In 1804, it became part of Alta California, which was founded in 1769 by Gaspar de Portolá and included California, Utah, and parts of Wyoming, Colorado, New Mexico, and Arizona. After Mexico's War of Independence in 1821, Alta California became a state of Mexico. Then, with the Mexican-American War of 1846–1848, the area was acquired by the United States. Subsequently, it became part of the Utah Territory and later became the Nevada Territory. In 1861, the Nevada Territory separated from the Utah Territory, and in 1864 Nevada became the 36th state.

The presence of Latinos in Nevada and other territories that constitute the United States precedes the arrival of the Pilgrims on the *Mayflower*. When the Pilgrims anchored in 1620 in Provincetown Harbor, Cape Cod, there were already settlements in Florida and the southwestern region, built by Spanish conquistadors and missionaries. The interactions between the Spaniards and the aboriginal population over more than 500 years have pushed Latinos to assume a protagonist role in the nation's history, one that has contributed enormously to its rich culture.

For centuries, the Iberian Peninsula had gone through *La Reconquista*. After centuries in which the three major Western religions—Christianity, Judaism, and Islam—coexisted, a centralized government ruled by the unlikely marriage of Ferdinand of Aragón and Isabel of Castile defined the nation in religious and military terms. The last Moorish stronghold to fall was Granada in 1492. Just as Columbus crossed the Atlantic in search of a new route to the Indies and stumbled in the process on a gigantic, previously unknown continent, there were edicts to expel the Jewish community. A few years later the Arabs would suffer a similar fate. The colonies across the Atlantic served a manifold purpose, including as sources of revenue and a landscape suitable for the expansionist Christian vision. The colonies included much of the Caribbean Basin, Florida, Mexico, Central America, a large portion of South America, and the Philippines too.

Over time the Catholic Church became the biggest owner of real estate in the Southwest. The biggest denominations were the Franciscans, the Dominicans, the Agustinians, and the Jesuits. The latter was responsible for educating large portions of the native population. Among the leading Jesuit educators was Father Eusebio Kino, a polymath (among other things, he was an astronomer, a cartographer, a geographer, and an explorer) whose work was primarily in the region known as

Primería Alta (modern-day Sonora in Mexico and southern Arizona in the United States). In total, Kino established two dozen missions. (In John Steinbeck's novel *The Pearl* [1947], a character is named after him.)

### Who was Alvar Núñez Cabeza de Vaca?

Among the most significant, and ill-fated, Spanish explorers, Alvar Núñez Cabeza de Vaca was the author of *La Relación* (1542). Known in English as the *Chronicle of the Narváez Expedition*, in this account he narrates his journey from Florida to the Southwest and back. As one of the members of the failed expedition of Pánfilo de Narváez, which foundered off the coast of Florida, he traveled for a decade, along and with other survivors of the shipwreck, coming across Indian tribes and passing for a healer in order to save his life. His narrative was drafted after his return to Spain, which explains why it has been contested as an untrustworthy historical document.

### What other types of "accounts" survive?

"Accounts" are chronicles of explorations produced during the colonial period. They include journals, diaries, travel writing, poems, and even plays, and they are about Florida, New Mexico, Arizona, Texas, California, and the Pacific Northwest. The adventures of the explorer Hernando de Soto were described by the Portuguese chronicler Caballero de Elvas in the 1551 book *True Relation of the Vicissitudes That Attended the Governor Don Hernando de Soto and Some Nobles of Portugal in the Discovery of the Province of Florida Now Just Given by a Fidalgo of Elvas*, as well as by El Inca Garcilaso de la Vega, a mestizo known for the account *La Florida del Inca* (1605). As well, de Soto's personal secretary, Rodrigo Rangel, authored the *Diario de Rodrigo Ranjel*.

Alonso Gregorio de Escobedo wrote an epic poem with valuable ethnographic information, titled *La Florida* (in English it is known as *Pirates, Indians, and Spaniards*). Fray Marcos de Niza, one of the first explorers of New Mexico, kept an influential diary about Arizona that inspired future adventurers to embark on similar journeys. His quest, which ended in disaster when his 300 men were killed by Zuni Indians, was to find the fabled Seven Cities of Cibola. Among those inspired by de Niza were Francisco Vázquez de Coronado, whose journey to New Mexico, Texas, and Kansas between 1540 and 1542 was told by Pedro Castañeda de Nájera in *The Narrative of the Expedition of Coronado*.

The journey of Juan de Oñate to New Mexico was told by Gaspar Pérez de Villagrá, a Creole who joined the expedition. His poem, composed in octosyllabic meter, is titled *Historia de la Nueva México* and was published in 1610. There are also works about Texas by Juan Bautista Chapa Historia del Nuevo Reino de León de 1650 a 1690 and Fray Juan Agustín Morfi Relación geográfica e histórica de la provincia de Texas o Nuevas Filipinas, 1673–1779. Juan Bautista de Anza explored northern Mexico and the San Francisco Bay area. Captain Juan Bautista de Anza's travels to Arizona and California were chronicled by Francisco Tomás Hermenegildo Garcés and Pedro Font. Other explorers include Juan Crespí, Fray Francisco Palóu, and Fray Junípero Serra. The latter was an evangelist who established almost two dozen missions still standing in California.

One might ask what happened to the aboriginal perspective. Unfortunately, there are no such documents. History, it is often said, is delivered from the viewpoint of the conquerors, not of the vanquished. Missionaries sometimes went out of their way to express in their narratives the opinion of the indigenous populations. Even if these opinions were accurate, readers inevitably approach them with a degree of skepticism. After all, they had been filtered through someone else's perspective, especially because the bearers of news used all sorts of powerful strategies to extract the stories from the population they controlled.

## What was the function of the missions?

The missions were influential religious institutions, established during the colonial period to educate the aboriginal populations through Catholic instruction. There were missions in Florida, South Carolina, Georgia, Virginia, Alabama, Mississippi, Texas, New Mexico, California, Oklahoma, Utah, Nevada, and other states. Designed as self-sufficient enclaves that included water systems, schools, jails, ranches, and carpentries, first by Jesuits and then by Franciscans, they initially served the Spanish missionaries and complemented other institutions like presidios and pueblos.

The primary objective of these missions was the conversion of the Indians but they also had economic goals. It was hoped that the aboriginal population would be able to be turned into a solid labor force. There were different sorts of tasks: making pottery, raising cattle and other livestock, harvesting and processing wheat, among them. Religious instruction was delivered in Spanish, thus turning the missions into instruments of acculturation. Transgression of different kinds against Catholic values (theft, idolatry, sexual intercourse) were punishable, to various degrees, with prison, flagellation, and torture.

Compassion was one of their leitmotifs. The priests and other ecclesiastical figures used the missions to proselytize, but they also learned from the Indians. Fray Junípero Serra, for instance, learned aboriginal languages. Yet he was also harsh in his treatment of his pupils. To this day he remains a controversial figure, having converted to Catholicism close to 5,000 people. (Pope John Paul II beatified him.)

In spite of what is commonly assumed, the colonial effort in the New World was achieved with resistance from the native population. In the 17th century, the Seminoles rebelled in Florida, just as the Pueblo Indians did in New Mexico. At times these rebellions continued for stretches of time. Often there were runaway Indians escaping the harsh treatment. And in a more organized fashion, there were subversions such as the Pueblo Revolt of 1680 and the Chumash Revolt of 1824.

By the first part of the 19th century, after Mexico became independent and a wave of anticlericalism swept the northern territories, the system fell into disarray, as the population turned away from the Church.

Nowadays some of these missions are museums offering a window into the Spanish past. This transformation is welcome but not without its pitfalls. As a result of the legacy of abuse, repression, and colonialism, a strong anti-Spanish feeling subsists in Latino culture. Cyclically, this sentiment is heightened according to the needs of the time, as it did, for instance, during the Spanish-American War of 1898. It takes the form of resistance to contemporary Spanish life. These museums frequently pay tribute to the past, carefully avoiding reference to the consequences of that past, a strategy that feels like myopia. As controversial as it might be to address the contested legacy, at times it might be a better approach, inviting a way to create a bridge between the past, the present, and the future.

### Why did the Spanish Empire collapse?

It is often assumed that the Southwest became part of the United States as a result of annexation. Not quite, although this idea isn't altogether wrong. Per the cycle of Social Darwinism, empires rise and fall. As the Spanish Empire was crumbling down, the United States was on the rise as a world force. It embraced an expansionist ideology in the 19th century known as Manifest Destiny. Through annexations, military endeavors, and diplomatic maneuvering, it first took control of what is today the Southwest, then of Cuba, Puerto Rico, the Philippines, Hawaii, and Guam. It promised the inhabitants of those territories respect but quickly turned them into secondrate citizens. The United States ignored their landownerships, ridiculed their Spanish as a language of barbarism, and curtailed their labor and educational opportunities. The frustration ensured an eventual explosion of riots and organized activism.

### What kind of diplomatic relationship have Mexico and the United States had over time?

Nowhere else on the globe do more different civilizations share the same border. The countries represent haves and have-nots: the United States is a world power while Mexico is a developing country. One example among many is the clash, in early 2017, at the beginning of the Trump administration, between Donald Trump and Mexico's president, Enrique Peña Nieto, over the building of a wall across the border and who should pay for it. The tension, of course, was about immigration, legal and undocumented. At one point in that clash, President Trump, using his favorite form of communication, tweeted that a tariff of 20% should be applied to any Mexican import to the United States, which, in his own view, would indirectly cover the price of building the wall.

This statement needs to be seen in context. In terms of priority, the United States at the time was Mexico's first commercial partner, selling to it the largest percentage of its products. Conversely, Mexico was the United States' second largest partner. Neither could truly afford to break their economic partnership, yet President Trump was the one in a position of power.

At any rate, the relationship between the two nations has been defined by utilitarianism. It has gone through periods of harmony and misunderstanding and even violence. The border dividing the two countries is a result of push-and-pull policies. It came about in the middle of the 19th century, as the United States was undergoing a Western expansion justified by the policy of Manifest Destiny.

### Has the Rio Grande always served as the divide?

Americans call the river that runs along the border between the United States and Mexico the Rio Grande; Mexicans refer to it Río Bravo del Norte. (*Bravo* in Spanish means strong, restless.) Throughout history the river, which is some 1,885 miles long and was designated as one of the American Heritage Rivers in 1997, also had diverse appellations among the indigenous people. For instance, the Pueblo and Navajo people called it in five different ways: *mets'ichi chena*, "Big River"; *posoge*, "Big River"; *paslápaane*, "Big River"; *hañapakwa*, "Great Waters"; and *Tó Ba'áadi*, Navajo, "Female River."

There is a rich mythology surrounding the river. For the people who have lived next to it, it has been seen, variously, as a protective mother, a door to alternative realities, and as the bellwether for the overall health of the environment in the region. People fear it and they pray to it. This plethora of reactions is depicted in folktales, songs, poems, children's stories, novels, TV, plays, and movies.

Cabeza de Vaca apparently crossed it in 1535. Francisco Vázquez de Coronado did the same in 1540. Nevertheless, it didn't become a binational border until the Treaty of Guadalupe Hidalgo in 1848. In fact, a large portion of the river was not even mapped out until this time. It was remapped again in 1853–1854, when the Gadsden Purchase took place.

### What kind of border existed before?

Prior to the current delineation, Mexico, which achieved its independence in 1821 in a rebellion against Spanish rule led by a priest named Miguel Hidalgo y Costilla, controlled a large portion of what are today the southwestern territories of the United States. Yet the boundaries weren't strictly marked. That year Mexico took possession of California, which had also been under Spanish rule. Also that year, it allowed Stephen F. Austin, the Virginia-born impresario who is known as the "Father of Texas," to settle about 300 American families in the region. That agreement opened up a series of conflicts between the two countries, giving Texas the excuse of breaking ties with Mexico. Other Anglos settled along what is currently the border during the American Civil War and the California Gold Rush. Ultimately, the border took its present form in 1848.

## How did Latinos do under an independent Texas?

The Republic of Texas declared its independence from Mexico in 1835, consummating it as such on March 2, 1836. It also bestowed citizenship on those living within its borders, including Mexicans. The constitution of 1845 confirmed this status for *tejanos*, as Mexicans from the region are known. In reality their situation was less than equal. Although *tejanos* of the political elite more or less retained their status under the new, independent government, the majority of Mexicans were treated as second-rate citizens, their culture oppressed by Anglo rulers. Over time, this racial strife has segregated Latinos in the state.

## What happened at the Alamo?

The Battle of the Alamo wasn't the most significant in Texas's campaign for independence. But, along with the Goliad Massacre, it allowed Texas a moral victory, ultimately leading to the Battle of San Jacinto, between the forces of Sam Houston and those of General Antonio López de Santa Anna.

Over time, the Alamo has become a tourist destination. Originally, it was a series of buildings in the Mission of San Antonio de Valero, which was founded in 1691. The answer to the question of what happened at the Alamo depends on what side of the conflict you study. Through media and history books, the outcome has acquired mythical, one might say even martyrological, proportions. The performance of American soldiers has become the subject of legend while the role *tejanos* played on the Texan side has been eclipsed and even ignored. Ironically, the fact that the Mexican army won the battle has become irrelevant. For nationalistic reasons, what matters, it seems, is that a small group of David-like, fervent fighters defended their fort against an aggressive, Spanish-speaking Goliath.

## What are the facts of the Battle of the Alamo?

When Texas declared its independence, General López de Santa Anna ordered several thousand soldiers (the exact number remains unknown, although accounts put the number anywhere from 5,000 to 10,000) to fight Sam Houston's separatists. In late 1835, the Texan forces captured the Alamo and stationed some 200 men in it under the leadership of Colonel William Barret Travis. The Mexicans bombarded the place with heavy artillery in the early days of March 1836. Aware of the impending doom, Trevis gathered his people, asking them if they were willing to leave before the fight started. Lore has it that nobody chose to leave, although historians have actually uncovered the story of one soldier who did. A bloody one-on-one battle took place on March 6th, resulting in the deaths of 1,000 Mexicans and everyone on the Texan side, including Colonel James (Jim) Bowie and David (Davy) Crockett. A decade later, between 1846 and 1848, Mexico and the United States would engage, once again, in war.

## How is the Alamo portrayed in art?

The representations are plentiful, from John Wayne's dud of a film (*The Alamo* [1960]) and John Ford's *Two Rode Together* (1961), to novels about the battles and the various protagonists, diaries, historical accounts, scholarly investigations, posters, postal stamps, children's and young adult books, and comic strips. The material is almost always patriotic. Purportedly the phrase "Remember the Alamo!" came from one of the volunteers in Sam Houston's army in the Battle of San Jacinto. Whether true or false, so invested were the victors in the telling of such episodes that there surely is no easy way to forget the battle. Of course, the questions are what ought to be remembered? And by whom?

### What was the cause of the Mexican-American War?

The causes date back to the time when President James Monroe, in his second inaugural address, laid out what would become the Monroe Doctrine. The doctrine established a policy of non-intervention of European countries in the Americas. This was a bold move by the young American nation to defy political power from the Old World. Ultimately, it became something altogether different: a justification for the United States to insert itself in the affairs of other nations this side of the Atlantic Ocean. That justification is embedded in the concept of Manifest Destiny.

Essentially, the Mexican-American War was the result of the United States' westward expansionist drive, to reach "from sea to shining sea." (Interestingly, the song "America the Beautiful" was written almost 50 years later, in 1893, by Katherine Lee Bates while she was teaching at Colorado College and after she went on a trip to the 14,000-foot Pikes Peak, first on a wagon and then on mules. When she reached the top, she obviously never saw the sea but "a sea-like expanse," which made her think of the nation's edges.)

### Were there other causes?

Slavery was also a factor. In the 1840s, less than a decade after Texas declared its independence from Mexico, US attention turned to the question of Texas becoming part of the Union. The debate was particularly loud among pro- and antislavery advocates. President James Polk pushed for an annexation, which in turn created a border conflict with Mexico because the United States wanted the border to be on the Rio Grande, while Mexico believed it should be some 32 miles to the north, at the Río Nueces. *Nueces*, in Spanish," means nuts.

### How did Mexico react to the annexation of Texas?

At the time Mexico was going through some political insta-bility. When in 1845 an American envoy was refused entry,

President Polk asked General Zachary Taylor to send troops to the southern Texas border and to secure some ports on the Gulf of Mexico. Mexico reacted by militarizing the border as well. A tense period ensued, until Mexican General Mariano Arista dispatched a battalion across the river. The United States was incensed and declared war in early May 1846.

### How did the war shape up?

US troops, under the command of Zachary Taylor, invaded Mexico in 1846. They first advanced toward Matamoros and then took possession of Monterrey. General Santa Anna waited for them in the town of Buena Vista with tens of thousands of troops. Again, the Americans were victorious. Another military endeavor attacked Tampico, in the Gulf of Mexico. In control of northern Mexico, the Americans marched with confidence toward Mexico City and raised the US flag in the capital on September 14, 1847.

### Were Americans supportive of the effort?

Not really. The effort was quite unpopular because it required a tax increase, the income from which was invested in military arsenal and other warlike needs. It was actually perceived as "Mr. Polk's War," as the public believed that President Polk instigated it in the interest of expanding slavery in the United States. Lack of support forced the administration to strike a deal with the Mexican government to finish the war.

### What was the Treaty of Guadalupe Hidalgo about?

Negotiated by the chief clerk of the State Department and signed on February 2, 1848, its purpose was to bring an end to the military confrontation. But the treaty, which stands as one of the largest transfers of land from one country to another in world history, was defined by the Americans, since they were the victors.

## What was agreed?

The treaty concluded the war, and it forced Mexico to sell more than half of its territory to the United States. This land included the states of New Mexico, Arizona, California, Utah, Colorado, Nevada, and parts of Wyoming. It was supposed to include a provision that protected Mexicans in those territories, but the United States eliminated the relevant article, and Mexicans lost their land as a result. The Mexican government asked the United States to reconsider this provision, and the two countries signed the Querétaro Protocol. Eventually, the Americans rejected that treaty as well.

## What was the Gadsden Purchase about?

Also known as the Tratado de Mesilla, the Gadsden Purchase Treaty was signed on December 30, 1853, five years after the Treaty of Guadalupe Hidalgo. In it Mexico officially ceded 30,000 square miles of southern Arizona and New Mexico for $10 million. The name comes from James Gadsden, whom President Franklin Pierce appointed as minister to Mexico. Originally the United States was interested in buying Baja California, Sonora, and other land, but Mexico refused to sell. Armies were again mobilized. In the end Washington only got the region of the Mesilla, which is rich in minerals.

## How did Mexico react to the loss?

Mexicans have a love-hate relationship with the United States. While tourism, trade, and immigration link them inseparably, the view from across the Rio Grande is that Americans are at once arrogant and gullible, pretending to be peacekeepers when in fact their drive is unquestionably imperialistic.

The Mexican-American War is deeply ingrained in collective Mexican memory as an embarrassing disaster that solidified its neighbor's mighty power. Mexicans talk about Moctezuma's revenge, a time in the future when there will be an opportunity to regain what was taken away by *el coloso del norte*. (Moctezuma's revenge is also a reference to the stomach ailments that travelers get as a result of drinking contaminated water. By the way, variant spellings of the name in the 19th century included Montezuma, Moteczoma, Motecuhzma, Moteuczomah, and Mwatazuma.) Equally painful is its place in Chicano history, where the Treaty of Guadalupe Hidalgo in particular is seen as a double betrayal: from Mexico, a weak country incapable of recognizing the value of its northern provinces; and from the United States, a colonizing force whose interest in the native population of the region was minimal.

### What role did Spain have in the Southwest after 1848?

A remote one at best. Throughout the 19th century, the Spanish Empire slowly crumbled, ultimately falling during the Spanish-American War. The conflict forced its dwellers in the peninsula to go through a challenging period of introspection.

### What was the Spanish-American War about?

Among other names, in Spanish it is called *"la Guerra del 98"* because it took place in 1898. This was the last salvo of the Spanish Empire before its collapse. Spain lost control of Cuba, Puerto Rico, and the Philippines, among other places. In time some of them entered the orbit of the United States, which was the ascending empire at the end of the 19th century.

The Spanish-American War shook the essence of the Hispanic world. It came at a time when the wars of independence from Spain had reached a climax, seemingly occurring through a domino effect. Yet Spain remained adamant about its control of some territories across the Atlantic. In Madrid and other cities in the Iberian Peninsula, intellectuals like Miguel de Unamuno, José Ortega y Gasset, and others talked of a "depressive" state of mind in the overall population. By contrast, intellectuals from Latin America such as José Martí, Rubén Darío, and others—who saw themselves as part of a movement called *Modernismo*—believed in a social, political, and cultural renewal. As part of it, they rejected Iberian influences, looking instead to France for inspiration.

One of the most renowned *Modernistas* was the Uruguayan essayist José Enrique Rodó, who published the book *Ariel* in 1900. Using Shakespeare's last play, *The Tempest*, as his urtext, and concentrating on two characters, Ariel and Caliban, he delivered an indictment of the United States as a materialist, utilitarian nation, whereas he portrayed Latin America as spiritual and pragmatic. By the way, this is also the age of Positivism, a philosophical trend that endorsed scientific thinking, logic, and rationality and repelled faith and superstition.

### What were the factors leading to that war?

At this time, anti-Spanish sentiment took shape in the United States (where it more or less continues unabated). The Iberian Peninsula was portrayed in William Randolph Hearst's *New York Journal-American* (1937–1966) and Joseph Pulitzer's *New York World* (1860–1931) as politically awkward and even stagnant, its population uneducated. These perceptions also colored Spain's former colonies, which Americans perceived as barbaric. (Ironically, the Pulitzer Prizes that recognize artistic and journalistic achievements are named after Pulitzer. They were established in 1917 with money he bequeathed to Columbia University.) This view was underscored by the ingrained conviction that the United States was called to play a larger role on this side of the Atlantic through the ideology of Manifest Destiny, which justified any territorial takeover in its orbit. Such beliefs led to the military confrontation with Spain.

## What started it?

Since 1868, at the time of the "Ten-Year War," Cuba had struggled for independence from Spain. The movement achieved momentum in 1895 as a series of revolutionary leaders, including Antonio Maceo, Máximo Gómez, and José Martí, arrived on the island and orchestrated an insurgent fight. Martí, born in 1853 in Havana, has been turned into a hero, worshiped for his anticolonialism, his views on racial and cultural diversity, and his courage to oppose imperial powers. He was an intellectual who authored essays and travel pieces he dispatched to newspapers in Latin America. He also wrote a children's book called *La edad de oro* (The golden age [1889]) and is principally known through his poems, including *Versos sencillos* (1891), on which the Cuban song "*Guantanamera*" is based. Today the iconography about him is extensive, both on the island and outside. He was killed on May 19, 1895, in one of those early battles. The Spanish army responded by removing support for the rebels in the countryside. The strategy was called "reconcentration." It forced Cubans into Spanish-controlled cities, but it also precipitated an outbreak of epidemics, hunger, and chaos. The military encounters between the colonial forces and the rebels were cruel. American and other foreign interests were destroyed.

In the United States, public opinion turned against Spain for its failure to control the insurgents but soon oscillated in the other direction, creating sympathy for the rebels.

## Why was it called the Spanish-American War?

The name is a misnomer. The United States was considering involvement in the conflict when the battleship USS *Maine*, anchored in Havana "to protect the lives and property of American citizens there," exploded on February 15, 1898. More than 260 sailors on board were killed. It is still unclear what caused the explosion but a naval inquiry suggested that

Spain was responsible. President William McKinley reacted by organizing a military intervention, initially by blockading some Cuban ports. Spain was furious and declared war on the United States, as Congress approved the sending of troops. For all this, the name should be the Spanish-Cuban-American War. A more suitable appellation is the War of '98.

### How did the conflict evolve?

A military escalation diversified the fronts on both American coasts. The Philippines and Guam, in the Pacific Ocean, were also under Spanish rule, and the United States was interested in them.

In Cuba, the Americans landed on territory controlled by the revolutionary forces. They marched toward Santiago, then toward the south. The battles were fierce, and an epidemic of yellow fever spread on both sides. Finally, the Spanish surrendered its 22,000 troops on July 17, 1898.

### What about Hawaii?

Eventually, the island, which at the time was politically unstable already, a pattern that unfortunately has become a sine qua non throughout its history, was invaded by the American army. This happened in 1915, when Theodore Roosevelt, amending the Monroe Doctrine, occupied the island.

Puerto Rico was seized too in 1898. It started with an invasion that landed in Guánica, in the southern island. By the early 20th century, the United States and Puerto Rico were engaged in a relationship of colonization.

### Who were the Rough Riders?

The Rough Riders were a volunteer cavalry unit led by Theodore Roosevelt, who nurtured dreams of one day becoming president of the United States. The unit captured San Juan Hill and the fort of El Caney on July 1, 1898.

## What was the outcome of the war?

The Spanish Empire, and to a lesser extent Portugal and France, ruled the Americas between 1492 and 1898. By the beginning of the 20th century, the United States had emerged as the uncontested regional superpower, controlling not only the entire land from Maine to Florida, and over to California and Oregon, but also the Philippine archipelago, Guam, Hawaii, and Puerto Rico. Under the Platt Amendment, it was also allowed to have an army base in Guantánamo, Cuba.

## What happened with Cuba and Puerto Rico after Spain seceded from the Caribbean Basin?

Before the war, the Teller Amendment, approved by Congress, established that the United States was forbidden "to exercise sovereignty, jurisdiction, and control [over Cuba] . . . except the pacification thereof." In the end, the peace agreement, known as the Treaty of Paris of 1898, was negotiated between Spain and the United States, but not Cuba. A US-controlled military government, under the direction of General John R. Brooke, ruled Cuba between 1898 and 1902. And in 1902, a US-supported president, Tomás Estrada Palma, was inaugurated.

Puerto Rico's situation was different. After the war, the United States established a military government on the island. Then came the Foraker Act, signed into law in 1900, in which it was established that the American president at the time, McKinley, with the advice of the Senate, would be responsible for selecting the island's governor. The governor's term would be four years, but the US president would have the right to replace him at any point.

### Why was the Jones-Shafroth Act signed?

For more than 15 years, at the outset of the 20th century, Puerto Rico existed under total American control. Finally, in 1917, the US Congress enacted the Jones-Shafroth Act, giving citizenship to Puerto Ricans and allowing them to democratically elect their legislature. The island, thereafter defined as a commonwealth (in Spanish, *estado libre asociado*), remains under American power. That status has proven to be astonishingly controversial, over time dividing the political establishment, the intellectual elite, and even the population at large into three groups: those supporting the current status, those advocating independence from the United States, and those endorsing a change to full statehood under the US constitution. The architects of the current status include the poet, journalist, and politician Luis Muñoz Marín, who with his Popular Democratic Party worked closely with the United States to create the island's constitution, bringing about economic and political stability, and Luis A. Ferré, a businessman, art patron, founder of the New Progressive Party, and governor, who in 1968 brought down the dominance of Muñóz Marín's Popular Democratic party and established a line of statehood-proponent leaders.

### Did Latinos play a role in the two world wars?

Latinos played a small but defining role in World War I. Records are scarce but Latino soldiers saw combat during the war. For many from Texas and other states, serving in the military was their first experience with mainstream US society. Far more participated in World War II, when an estimated 375,000 Latinos served in the armed forces. Among them, some 65,000 were Puerto Ricans. They fought valiantly. Among other recognitions, they received twelve Medals of Honor. Still, the period was one of intolerance. The Sleepy Lagoon Case and the Zoot Suit Riot instigated stereotypes and led to widespread racism. As Latinos were enlisting and fighting on the battlefield, those on the home front were vulnerable to verbal and sometimes physical abuse. The Bracero Program also contributed to the war by placing millions of Mexicans in factories. But there was a sense among some in the United States that Mexicans were "taking away American jobs," and this alienated Mexicans and put them in a difficult position. Eventually, the soldiers enrolled in the armed forces became agents of change. They benefited from the G.I. Bill of Rights and, as they became veterans, enrolled in college and bought new homes. A generation of business and political leaders emerged out of it.

### What were the circumstances of the Sleepy Lagoon Case?

The case resulted from an incident on August 2, 1942, when 22-year-old José Díaz, a Mexican American, was stabbed near Sleepy Lagoon, a water-filled gravel pit in Los Angeles. He died later that day. The circumstances of his death remain unclear but the incident triggered a wave of police harassment against Mexican Americans. The Los Angeles Police Department eventually arrested 600 youngsters of Mexican descent, charging 22 with having been involved in the crime.

### What role did the media play in the agitation?

The Sleepy Lagoon Case wasn't only tried in the courtroom. The media in Los Angeles, from the *Times* to the *Herald Express* and the *Daily News*, was also deeply involved. Stereotypes about rowdy, brawling Pachucos were played out in the news on a regular basis. World War II was taking place in Europe, and the United States focused internally on ethnic groups the mainstream judged as dangerous.

Historians have shown the degree to which the trial itself was biased. The defendants were not allowed to consult with their lawyers. They were also forced to keep the same clothes they were wearing or to shave and cut their hair. Judge Charles Fricke, in charge of the case, often described the defendants as gangsters, while the prosecution described all Mexican

Americans as cowards. Even though there was a lack of evidence connecting the defendants to the murder, the verdict, announced on January 1943, declared 17 of them guilty of second-degree murder, assault, or criminal conspiracy. Ten were sent to San Quentin Prison.

To this day, the Sleepy Lagoon Case is fixed in Latino memory as an incident of police abuse and misguided justice. More than anything, it remains an example of the fragile place Mexican Americans have in American society.

### What were the Zoot Suit Riots about?

In the early 1940s, just as the United States was fighting fascism in Europe, a drive to identify and eradicate alien, potentially dangerous elements in society took place internally. One example is the xenophobic outburst that targeted Japanese Americans after Pearl Harbor. Likewise, Mexican Americans were regularly vilified in the media and, on occasion, physically attacked. One such attack took place on Main Street in East Los Angeles on June 3, 1943. Eleven white sailors alleged that they were harassed by a group of Spanish speakers dressed in zoot suits, a clothing style consisting of baggy pants, wide-brimmed hats, and shiny leather shoes. The L.A. Police Department was called to clear the area. A day later some 200 navy recruits arrived in the neighborhood in 20 taxicabs and beat a Zoot Suiter, a term used to describe a Pachuco. The violence continued for four days. Businesses were looted and Mexican Americans were stripped of their clothes and humiliated in public. African Americans were also targeted. No one was killed, but the riots soon spread to San Diego, Detroit, Baltimore, and Philadelphia.

### Does the understanding of history for Latinos change after World War II?

The "common past" of Latinos more or less ends in 1950, when a number of incidents prompted an emphasis on national histories. Among them were violent outbursts that took place in the 1940s, such as the Sleepy Lagoon Case and the Zoot Suit Riots. These were antecedents to the Chicano movement and help explain the movement's rise. For that matter, even leaders like Cesar Chavez, Dolores Huerta, and Reies López Tijerina saw the Treaty of Guadalupe Hidalgo as the foundation to the labor and civil rights struggle that came in the second half of the 20th century.

Another way of looking at the "common past" is as a period of awakening. It not only held the seeds of what was to come, but also showed signs of the emerging minority that is often called "the sleeping giant."

# 3

# THE SLEEPING GIANT

*Are Americans in general aware of the way Latinos
as a minority are a sum of parts?*

The Latin motto of the United States, *e pluribus unum*, about
which I reflected earlier, was established in 1776, the year of
the nation's independence. It has remained a kind of rationale
for social life ever since, first as a reference to the 13 colonies
uniting under one banner, then the constellation of 13 stars.
Over time it has been taken to mean an endorsement of plu-
ralism. Latinos themselves are also a multiplicity, a sum of
parts. People of different backgrounds have converged in a
single space and are shaping a dynamic identity. It has taken
some time for non-Latinos to recognize this phenomenon.
There needs to be a debunking of stereotypes, for no society is
free from stereotypes but only a free and intellectually curious
one is able to challenge them. *E pluribus unum* exemplifies the
sum of parts at the heart of Latino civilization.

*Do Latino loyalties follow party lines?*

The heterogeneity of Latinos is evident across the map.
Demographically, they concentrate in western and southern states and gather together in major cities. Economically,
a vast majority of Latinos lives under the poverty level. The
Democratic Party used to be supported by Mexican Americans

and Puerto Ricans while Cuban Americans sympathized with the Republican Party. Issues like abortion, the death penalty, national security, US-Latin American relations, and gay marriage have complicated these loyalties. While the Voting Rights Act of 1965 made it possible for Latinos to have a wider representation, it didn't reconfigure party loyalties. On the contrary, these loyalties were strengthened.

Claims that the Republican Party is engaged in gerrymandering surface cyclically during every presidential and midterm election. Conversely, the Democratic Party, while supporting Latinos, doesn't appear to make room for them at the leadership level. The immigration marches of 2006 galvanized a minority in search of political leadership. In fact, in the 2016 presidential election, it was the Republican Party that showcased a couple of early forerunners: Ted Cruz and Marco Rubio.

### In general, how active are Latinos in politics?

Latino participation in politics is intense, despite decades of alienation. Power used to be polarized. For decades the centers of gravity were in the Southwest, among Mexican Americans, and on the East Coast, among mainland Puerto Ricans in New York and Cuban Americans in Florida. Although there were bridges between them, each national group responded to its own needs and aspirations. The demographic growth of the groups during the late 20th century simultaneously brought about a concentration and a dispersion of power. Under the rubric of "Latino," a new approach to ethnic politics took shape. The need to agglutinate different interests into a single voice allowed for a more powerful national political platform.

According to specialists, Latinos constitute "the shock of the new" in the American political landscape. They have yet to acknowledge the full scope of their political clout but when they do, they are likely to be decisive in determining the country's fate. The barriers to decisive political participation are marginalization and enfranchisement. Can Latinos wake up as a homogenized constituency? Can a single national leader galvanize Latinos? Is political homogeneity possible?

### Do Latinos vote?

This question is central to the contested presidential election in 2016 between Hillary Clinton and Donald Trump. As the crucial date of the election approached, Latinos were portrayed by the media and the political establishment as "the sleeping giant about to wake up." But while participation was indeed higher than anything seen before at the national level, it was also less than predicted. Clinton got 68% of the Latino vote and Trump, 28%. This was in line with the 2008 presidential election, when Barack Obama won 67% of the Latino vote and John McCain got 31%. But it fell short when compared to 2012, when Obama won 71% and Mitt Romney earned 27%.

Actually, given Trump's repeated attacks against Mexicans and Puerto Ricans and his talk of building a wall across the US-Mexico border, the fact that 28% of Latinos voted for him is significant. This number needs to be broken down by states, where it becomes clear that their endorsement of him was based on certain pledges, in contrast to the reason the same Latino voters disliked him. In Arizona, for instance, Latino voters endorsed Trump's promise of job formation while disregarding his statements about building the wall.

The issue of the Latino vote is directly connected with political representation. In political terms, for centuries Latinos as a minority were disenfranchised. It wasn't until the return of soldiers from World War II that the issue of representation took hold among Latinos. These soldiers' willingness to sacrifice their lives for the country made people realize that an active political life is crucial to bring about change. A number of organizations promoting participation were created in the late 1950s but a true impetus came about in 1965, with the Voting Rights Act (VRA), which allowed for a larger number of Latinos to have political representation. Signed by President Lyndon B. Johnson, the VRA also gave a boost to African Americans, Asians, and other ethnic groups traditionally marginalized from the political process. It prohibited any "standard, practice, or procedure" that could result "in denial or abridgment of the right of any citizen of the United States to vote on account of race or color." Subsequently, Congress made amendments, including one signed in 1975 that enfranchised "minority-language citizens" without full access to English. The amendment requires that bilingual ballots be made available in areas where a minority vote exceeds 5% of the overall vote.

In spite of the VRA, the percentage of Latinos who vote remains small. For example, according to the Federal Election Commission, 44.4% of qualified Latinos registered to vote in 1972, but only 2,103,000, or 37.5% of the population, voted that year. In 2002, 30 years later, only 32.6% of qualified Latinos registered to vote and the number that actually voted came to 4,747,000, only 18.9% of the population.

Numbers continue to change. In 2016, 27.3 million Latinos were eligible to cast ballots. This represented 12% of all eligible voters in the United States and was approximately four million more than in 2012. Interestingly, 44% of Latinos eligible to vote were millennials. In general, Latino voters turned out in high numbers, and they also went early to the booths. This was the case in Florida, where their early vote numbers increased by nearly 90% from 2012. However, the actual overall number of Latinos who voted in 2016 ended up being between 13.1 million to 14.7 million, meaning that a portion stayed home and didn't participate in the election.

### What are the reasons Latinos don't register or vote?

Apathy and a sense that the ethnic vote in general, and the Latino vote in particular, don't matter are major factors that continue to generate a feeling of disenfranchisement.

Throughout the decades, interviews and exit polls—frequently done by Spanish-speaking media and polling agencies—offer a gamut of emotions in this regard. People talk about the lack of candidates at the federal, state, and local levels who come from the Latino minority, that is, who look, think, and act like the majority of Latinos.

### How does race affect participation?

Traditionally, the black portion of the Latino electorate tends to identify with African American issues while the white portion oscillates more toward the mainstream. The Census Bureau started identifying the minority in 1980, when it counted 14,608,673 Latinos among the nation's more than 226 million citizens, or 6.4% of the total population. The numbers grew to 9% in 1990 and 12.5% in 2000. In 2000 there were 35,305,818. By 2010, there were more than 50,477,594 Latinos in the United States. And in 2015 that number was above 55 million, plus an estimated 11 million of undocumented immigrants. By then the Bureau was also distinguishing between white and nonwhite Latinos. And it had created another important category: people of mixed race. This categorization offers a clear picture of racial differences with the Latino minority.

### And economic status?

Class may well be the most decisive category defining the Latino vote. In 2014, 42.9% of Latinos in the United States earned less than $20,000; 40.3% earned between $20,000 and $49,000; and 16% earned more than $50,000. In other words, poverty is an impending problem with a plethora of ramifications.

### Who were the Latino political luminaries?

The deep roots of Mexican Americans explain the depth of their political tradition. For some those roots are grounded in their centuries-old life in the Southwest while for others it is connected with labor programs dating back to the early half of the 20th century.

The number of prominent political figures from the community has been relatively small, though. One of the heroes of the Texas revolution, who also had a role in the slave trade, was Juan Nepomuceno Seguín. In California, the influential Roybal family from Los Angeles, which included Edward and Lucille Roybal-Allard, who played important roles in representing Mexican American issues in the state while serving on city councils in Los Angeles and in the House of Representatives and Congress in the middle of the 20th century. Only after World War II did more faces attract the spotlight, although to this day the number remains small.

### Are there pan-Latino leaders?

During the civil rights era, Cesar Chavez, along with Dolores Huerta, Reies López Tijerina, and Rodolfo "Corky" González, represented Chicano migrant workers. Figures like José "Cha-Cha" Jiménez of the Puerto Rican Young Lords and Jorge Mas Canosa of the Cuban American National Foundation fulfilled a similar role in their respective national groups. In any case, nobody has been able to represent Latinos as a whole. Among Democrats, Joaquín and Julián Castro, identical twins, are important. One served as the Secretary of Housing and Urban Development in the Obama administration, while the other served as a city councilman and mayor in San Antonio.

Although the number remains small, there have been Latino senators, congressmen, representatives, and state figures. None has ever achieved iconic stature, though. An individual with the scope of influence enjoyed by Reverend Jesse Jackson among African Americans or Elie Wiesel among Jews has yet to materialize. A reason for this might be the fact that Latinos still feel a strong attachment to their national background. This at times impedes building bridges across national backgrounds. For instance, support by Mexican Americans for a Cuban American politician remains elusive and the same goes for the other way around.

Of course, a revered figure is Supreme Court Justice Sonia Sotomayor, who is of Puerto Rican descent. She relates her journey from the New York projects to the highest court in the land in her book *My Beloved World* (2013). Although not a politician (she has never been elected to public office), her left-leaning views on the law—she shares views with Justices Ruth Bader Ginsburg and Elena Kagan—align her with the majority of Latinos, who identify as liberals.

### What are the most prominent Latino political organizations?

The League of United Latin Americans Citizens was formed in 1921 in Corpus Christi, Texas, and it is the oldest Latino political organization in the country. It is a lobbying group engaged in literacy and citizen awareness programs, forging corporate alliances, making technology accessible to low-income people, housing, and immigration. There are also the Congressional Hispanic Caucus and the National Association of Latino Elected and Appointed Officials. The former was founded in 1976 by five Latino Democrats in Congress, including Herman Badillo. The group's objective is to use legislative channels to promote Latino issues. The latter was created the same year and seeks to increase political participation and to implement programs concerned with education, immigration, and community leadership.

In contrast, smaller, nationality-defined organizations are also active. Founded in 1968, during the Chicano movement, the National Council of La Raza originally known as the Southwest Council of La Raza congregates around Mexican American issues, even though it has attempted to go beyond its founding aims by representing Latinos in general. It has approximately 270 affiliates in about 40 states, including Puerto Rico. The National Puerto Rican Coalition, formed in 1977, is devoted to public policy issues connected with the Puerto Rican community. And the Cuban American National Foundation, founded in 1981, is a group with an objective to promote democratic change and a free-market economy in Cuba. There is also the Political Association of Spanish-Speaking Organizations formed in 1960, originally intended for the national stage but better known as an influential Texas organization. And the Council of Mexican-American Affairs, as well as the Mexican-American Political Association, the former established in 1953, the latter in 1959, are both devoted to improving the status of Mexican Americans. These are only five examples of Latino organizations with priorities defined by nationality. Understandably, their impact is less global and more concentrated.

### What are the traditional political loyalties of various national groups?

At the risk of simplification, overall, Mexicans and Central Americans, as well as Puerto Ricans, tend to lean toward the Democratic Party, whereas Cubans, especially those who came to the United States running from Fidel Castro's Cuba, affiliate with the Republican Party. But this equation often doesn't hold true: Ronald Reagan inspired left-leaning Latinos to switch sides, as did Donald Trump, though not in the same amount and with equal fervor. This ideological affiliation might be explained by looking at why immigrants from Latin America have moved to the United States. Many were running away from either economic strife or right-wing dictatorships.

### What kind of relationship has Cuba had with the United States?

After the Spanish-American War of 1898 and the mediated sovereignty that ensued until 1959, the island was a satellite of the United States. During the Gerardo Machado dictatorship and the Fulgencio Batista regime, the perception was that Cuba was a favorite place for American males to spend their money, on alcohol and women, in weekend escapades. The Platt Amendment, passed as part of the 1901 Army Appropriations Bill, gave Americans permission to intervene at will. For instance, there was a second occupation of the island by the United States between 1906 and 1909.

### Who was Gerardo Machado?

Gerardo Machado was a nationalist general in the Cuban war of independence who ran for president in Cuba in 1924 with the Liberal Party. Once in office, he protected Cuban goods but also remained close to the United States and persecuted and tortured the opposition. In 1930, in response to a massive strike, he suppressed constitutional rights.

### And Batista?

Batista was a seditious sergeant who led repeated coups and used puppet presidents to control power. In 1940 he ran successfully for president and at first promoted democratic principles. But when he lost reelection 12 years later, he organized another coup d'état. That coup stopped Fidel Castro during a campaign for the House of Representatives.

### Who was Fidel Castro?

No other politico in Cuba—and, arguably, in the whole of Latin America—has been more influential than Fidel Castro. Known from the 1960s until his death in 2016 as *el líder máximo*, Castro was the son of a wealthy landowner. He studied law but was fascinated by politics. His political aspirations frustrated by Batista, he filed a legal brief accusing him of corruption and simultaneously started to plan a rebellion. He was exiled in Mexico, where he met the Argentine lawyer Ernesto "Ché" Guevara. The two orchestrated the insurrection, which ultimately took place in Sierra Maestra in 1958. They marched triumphantly toward Havana as 1959 began.

Initially, Castro's ideology remained neutral. But by 1961 he declared himself a Marxist-Leninist and affiliated Cuba with the Soviet Bloc. Automatically, the island became a threat to the United States. President Kennedy was only one American president who sought to replace Castro, in this instance by staging a failed invasion in the Bay of Pigs. Others have tried to kill him. (There are suspicions that Castro was involved in the Kennedy assassination.) A commercial embargo was established against Cuba, first partially in 1960 by President Eisenhower, then totally in the Foreign Assistance Act of 1961.

Castro stayed in power until he resigned as president in 2008. His brother Raúl Castro replaced him as the island's supreme leader. Yet Fidel remained in control from behind the curtain. He survived 11 United States presidents and died at the age of 90 in 2016. By then President Barack Obama had already surrendered the idea of isolating Cuba because of its Communist ideology. He started an age of closer relations, which his successor, Donald Trump, has looked to undermine.

### *How did Fidel Castro's revolution impact Latin America?*

Castro's triumph was seen as a sign of resistance against a neighbor with a track history of foreign intervention. The Left supported Castro, and his ideology spread throughout the region. Having been offered a government post, "Ché" Guevara abandoned Cuba to fight for the liberation of Latin America. He was killed in Bolivia on October 9, 1967.

While Cuba was seen by other Latin American nations as an outlier in terms of state-established ideology, the region often coalesced to protest, to the degree possible, the United States' approach to it. In fact, it is acknowledged that it was at the urging of the first Latin American leader in the Vatican, the Argentina Jesuit priest Jorge Mario Bergoglio, *aka* Pope Francis, that Presidents Obama and Raúl Castro finally engaged in negotiations. This is a sign of the extent to which Latin America looked at Cuba as the valve of its relations with the United States.

### And the United States?

Since the late 1950s, Castro was portrayed in political circles and the mainstream media as a satanic force. During the civil rights movement, links between him and left-wing groups, while not overt, were commonly accepted. As time went by, not he but "Ché" was elevated to the status of folk hero. Guevara's image is ubiquitous in posters, movies, stamps, watches, and coffee mugs.

### What role did Latinos play during the Civil Rights era?

A struggle to give a voice to migrant workers in the Southwest took place in the 1960s, as part of the civil rights era. The regional labor force was predominantly from Mexico, a by-product of the Bracero Program implemented in the prior decades. The struggle came to be known as the Chicano movement. Its epicenter was California, although Texas, Arizona, Colorado, and New Mexico were important stages. Its principal leader was Cesar Chavez, a mestizo of humble background who rose to prominence by expounding a philosophy of nonviolence inspired by Mahatma Gandhi and the Reverend Martin Luther King Jr. Chavez and the United Farm Workers' union benefited from the activism of Dolores Huerta, Reies López Tijerina, and Rodolfo "Corky" González. *El movimiento* saw its vision crystallized in the *El plan espiritual de Aztlán*, as well as through the Treaty of Santa Bárbara.

One of the slogans of the era was "*El pueblo unido jamás será vencido,*" or "a united people shall never be defeated."

### What were the tenets of the Chicano Movement?

There is debate as to the exact dates of the Chicano movement, even though the decade of 1965 to 1975 is generally agreed to be the period of growth, consolidation, and early decline. Prior to 1965, most organizations representing Mexican Americans were started and controlled by middle-class individuals. These organizations included the League of United Latin American Citizens and the American G.I. Forum. Thus, the need to represent a more popular, grass-roots constituency was seen as important. By the time Cesar Chavez came along, these organizations focused on work-complaint strategies, such as marches, boycotts, plebiscites, and labor and hunger strikes.

Arguably, the Chicano movement remains the most influential of all political movements by and about Latinos in the United States. Its objectives, in general terms, were to improve the status of Mexican Americans in the country, from labor to health, from political participation to cultural integration. It also pushed for gender and racial equality as well as equal pay. But the truth is that it was never a homogeneous effort. There were those inside it that fought for secession, arguing that Chicanos lived under an American occupation dating back to the Treaty of Guadalupe Hidalgo. This argument was not in favor of returning to Mexico but of creating an autonomous, self-sufficient Chicano homeland. Others endorsed a more assimilationist approach, positing that the future of Mexican Americans was within the parameters of the United States per se.

### Who was Cesar Chavez?

Chavez is undoubtedly the most important Mexican American labor organizer of all time. His legacy still lives on in the form of a vindication of rights and the consolidation of an identity for Latinos of all backgrounds.

Born March 13, 1927, in Yuma, Arizona, Chavez came from a humble background. The second of five children, the family lived on a 160-acre farm, where they survived through agricultural work. Eventually the family moved to California in search of better opportunities but ended up as seasonal labor, picking cotton and carrots. Chavez's education was defined by his itinerant life. He once said that he attended some 65 different schools, some "for a day, a week, or a few months."

At the age of 19, he joined the Agricultural Workers' Union. He then served in the Navy for a couple of years during World War II, after which he returned to California.

### What was his intellectual inspiration?

After returning from the Navy, Chavez spent time reading. Eventually he discovered the work of Mahatma Gandhi, the Indian pacifist leader who advocated nonviolence as a strategy of protest and national recognition. Gandhi's approach marked Chavez deeply both as an organizer and as a conscientious objector. Through his leadership of the United Farm Workers he emphasized repeatedly that peaceful demonstrations were the only road toward recognition. And at the more personal level, he embraced hunger strikes, also inspired by Gandhi's attitude against the British rule in India before independence in 1948, as a way to denounce abuse and corruption. Chavez also modeled himself after his contemporary, the Reverend Martin Luther King Jr., another pacifist ethnic leader.

### How did Chavez become a union leader?

In 1952 Chavez met a community service organization leader named Fred Ross. Along with the Chicago-based organizer Saul Alinsky, Ross channeled Chavez's impetus and ideas. By the age of 33, Chavez was organizing families in the grape fields. Soon he was involved in the creation of the National Farm Workers Association. He used *la huelga*, or striking, as a strategy to get the grape owners to respond to workers' petitions.

### What is Chicanismo?

*Chicanismo* is an ideology about self-determination that uses the motifs of Mexican American life. Those leitmotifs include the myth of origins connected with Aztlán and the imagery of the pre-Columbian period, as well as the iconography of the Virgin of Guadalupe, the art and self-portraits of the painter Frida Kahlo, and the face and philosophy of the Argentine freedom-fighter Ernesto "Ché" Guevara. The ideology reached its apex in the 1960s and 1970s, as the Chicano movement unfolded, but its roots date back, albeit loosely, to the time of the signing of the Treaty of Guadalupe Hidalgo, and they remain alive to this day. More than an ideology, *Chicanismo* has become a philosophy that argues in favor of resisting mainstream American culture, emphasizing an alternative approach to public education as well as implementing social and political organizations devoted to improving the status quo of Mexican Americans in the United States.

### Where does the concept of la huelga come from?

In Spanish *la huelga* means the strike. It is a strategy to force business owners and authorities to attend to the plight of workers. In the pre-industrial age, farmers established alliances in order to protect their shared interests. In the 20th century, with the consolidation of capitalism and as the need to enlarge profits and revenues became tangible, workers sought other ways to fight for better working conditions. In the United States, strikes were an important protest tactic in the early part of the 20th century. In the 1920s and 1930s there were agricultural strikes in California. In 1933 alone, within a period of eight months, there were 33 strikes in the state. Cesar Chavez and the United Farm Workers successfully used *la huelga* to achieve their goals: the improvement of life and working conditions for Mexican American, Filipino, and other agricultural laborers. And he fasted.

### How long did an average fast last?

In 1968, he drank only water for 25 days. Another fast, this one for 24 days, took place in 1974. And in 1988, in the so-called Fast for Life, he lasted 35 days.

### Did religion play a role in Chavez's career?

His most enduring inspiration was his Catholic faith, which was a fixture in his childhood, strengthened through years of resistance. In speech after speech, Chavez talked of the power to be found in the patience and endurance of the faithful. He also established partnerships with religious figures who sympathized with the plight of the poor and oppressed Mexican labor workers. Even though the Catholic Church as such remained neutral to him, local priests in Arizona, New Mexico, and California joined the movement and supported public demonstrations.

### What is Chavez's legacy?

Chavez put his own life on the line in order to improve the situation of migrant workers. He tirelessly negotiated with grape owners and campaigned against pesticides. He used his fame and reputation to capture the attention of the average American by persuading people not to buy products produced through bad labor practices. In an age of civil disobedience, he became a folk hero. There are biographies, documentaries, picture books, and *corridos* inspired by him, as well as public schools, community centers, and streets named after him, particularly in the Southwest. And the Postal Service issued a stamp in his honor.

## When did he die?

Chavez died on April 23, 1993, in San Luis, Arizona. Some 50,000 people marched at his funeral. He is buried in La Paz, California, where the headquarters of the United Farm Workers are located. A foundation named after him was established at Glendale, also in California, in 1993, to keep his legacy alive.

A Chavez quote that summarizes his legacy is the following: "When we are perfectly honest with ourselves, we admit that our life is the only thing that belongs to us. Therefore, how we use our life is what determines the type of people we are."

## How should the concept of Aztlán be understood?

Aztlán is a crucial myth for Mexican Americans and was a source of inspiration during the Chicano movement. It is loosely based on history and contains biblical resonances.

According to lore, the founding of Mexico came about when the Aztecs, who emerged from the depths of the earth through seven caves and lived in a place called Aztlán—also spelled as Aztlatlán—were commanded to abandon their place, like the Canaanite patriarch Abraham. They were made to wander until a sign appeared before them: on a lake, an eagle devouring a serpent would be sitting on a cactus emerging from a stone. The sign would be proof that the land was theirs to settle. The image became a symbol engraved on Mexico's flag.

## Where is Aztlán located?

Myths are by definition elusive. The exact location of Aztlán is unknown. Some believe it is in the Mexican state of Nayarit, in the town San Felipe de Aztlán. Others locate it in the valley of the lower Colorado River. In historical time, the diaspora took place roughly in the first millennium AD. In Nahuatl the word "Aztlán" means "the land of the north" and "the land of white reeds." It could also be interpreted as "Place of Whiteness."

There is also the belief that the Aztec emperor Moctezuma II prophesized that his descendants, known as *la raza cósmica* or the Cosmic Race, would one day be called to conquer the earth. (This prophesy was explored, in pseudo-scientific terms, by a Mexican philosopher and Minister of Education, José Vasconcelos, in a 1927 essay, "*Mestizaje*.")

### Is Aztlán seen as an attainable homeland?

It is seen as elusive yet attainable. To Chicanos, whose connection to Mexico has always been through several degrees of separation, Aztlán is a utopian port of arrival and departure, a place first abandoned and then betrayed during the Treaty of Guadalupe Hidalgo and the Gadsden Purchase, then subsequently colonized by the United States. It is important to keep in mind that the civil rights era was also the age of anti-Vietnam demonstrations and, in general, of an anticolonial rhetoric. The myth of Aztlán must be understood as emerging from a debate on colonialism. Its recovery as a homeland for Chicanos ought to be seen in this context.

### What kinds of relationships were there between African Americans and Chicanos during the Civil Rights era?

Chicanos made partnerships with Filipino workers, as described further below. There was also a dialogue between Chavez and the Reverend Martin Luther King Jr. The importance of the Chicano movement to the civil rights era is still unacknowledged in textbooks. The civil rights era continues to be seen as a period of confrontation between blacks and whites against segregation, with little reference to the plight of other minorities.

### Who were the Puerto Rican Young Lords?

The Young Lords was originally a Chicago gang that, under the leadership of José "Cha-Cha" Jiménez, became a national activist organization seeking the social, economic, and political improvement of Puerto Ricans in the mainland United States. Their ultimate goal was the liberation of Puerto Rico. As a result of the concentration of Puerto Ricans, its prime stage was New York City, although they had branches in Philadelphia, Boston, Newark, New York, Connecticut, and Puerto Rico itself. They organized health tests, offered free food and clothes, made workshops about Puerto Rican history, and sought ways to persuade the New York City Board of Education to include Puerto Rican and Latino courses in the public school curriculum. They published a community-based newspaper called *Pa'lante*. They were also involved in "offensives," drives that at times resulted in the takeover of churches and hospitals.

The organization fell apart in 1972. In 1977, some of its former members hung a Puerto Rican flag over the crown of the Statue of Liberty, both to commemorate the independence of Puerto Rico and to denunciate its present colonial status.

### What role did Filipinos play in the Chicano Movement?

When the United Farm Workers Organizing Committee, AFL-CIO was formed in 1966 it resulted from a merger of the National Farm Workers Association and the Agricultural Workers Organizing Committee that enjoyed support and predominantly drew it's membership from the Filipino population. This is because Filipinos were also an important migrant labor component in the fields, involved in marches and strikes. They had come from the archipelago in search of a better life. A number of leaders working with Chavez were Filipino. Their ordeal is chronicled in Carlos Bulosan's autobiographical novel, *America Is in the Heart*.

### Who was Reies López Tijerina?

He was one of the significant figures of the movement. Reies López Tijerina was born in Falls City, Texas, although much of his work took place in New Mexico. He was a Pentecostal preacher and a leader of the Alianza Federal de las Mercedes, an alliance committed to reclaiming the lost real estate that resulted from the Treaty of Guadalupe Hidalgo.

Legal claims for lost property had been filed by individuals and in group cases but little had come out as a result. Then, on October 16, 1966, Tijerina led a one-week Alianza take-over of the Echo Amphitheater campground in Kit Carson National Forest, in Rio Arriba County. The place had been part of a Spanish estate during the 18th century. A while later they returned to take over the land and were arrested.

More Alianza meetings followed, as did confrontations with police and elected officials. In one such meeting, several Alianza members were arrested and jailed. A couple of days later, Tijerina and some supporters orchestrated a rescue operation. They also intended to make a citizen's arrest of the county district attorney, Alfonso Sánchez. A deputy sheriff and a state trooper were wounded. Soon the National Guard was hunting for Tijerina and his collaborators and, on June 10, 1967, they were captured. More than a year later, he success-fully defended himself in court.

He spent time in jail for other charges and then moved to the Mexican state of Michoacán. In the history of Latinos in the United States, he symbolizes the legal and also armed struggle for land rights dating back to the middle of the 19th century.

### How about Rodolfo "Corky" González?

González was an activist and author born in Denver, Colorado, in 1928. A Democrat who worked for the John F. Kennedy campaign, he ran for Denver City Council in 1955 but lost. His political career had taken off, though. He then enrolled with the neighborhood Youth Corps, which was a social program sponsored by Lyndon B. Johnson's administration. Through this he tried to increase Mexican American representation in the government. Along with 50 other people, he also walked out of the Equal Employment Opportunity Commission in 1966, claiming it had no Latino representative.

González is best known as the leader of the Crusade for Justice, an organization that promoted Latino empowerment. He also authored a myth-driven poem called *Yo Soy Joaquín/I Am Joaquín* (1967), in which he probed into the Chicano psyche. It became one of the banners of the Chicano movement. He also established a newspaper, *El gallo: La voz de la justicia*, and was a principal organizer of three youth conferences between 1969 and 1971, where *El plan espiritual de Aztlán* was drafted. Finally, he was a member of La Raza Unida party.

### What was El plan espiritual de Aztlán?

It was a manifesto drafted at the Chicano Liberation Youth Conference, held in Denver, in March 1969, at the Centro de la Crusada. The conference was attended by some 3,000 students from various Mexican American organizations and the Puerto Rican Young Lords. The rhetoric was militant, ethnocentric, civil rights–oriented, anticolonial, and nationalistic. González was instrumental in it. He was inspired by the myth of Aztlán. The manifesto called for the development of a working-class Chicano consciousness, separate from the rest of the nation.

The plan sought to develop unity, improve education, achieve economic self-determination, and defend Chicano interests. It also called for the restitution for lost property throughout history.

### What role did women play in the Chicano Movement?

Already in the early decades of the 20th century, during the Mexican Revolution, women—known as *las adelitas*—joined the troops, helping to cook and otherwise provide for the soldiers. This was at a time before feminism acquired momentum. The civil rights era in the United States also gave voice to the feminist movement. With leaders like Betty Friedan, Gloria Steinem, and others, the message for gender equality reached the wider population. This struggle became evident among Chicanos as women, equally employed as migrant labor, raised their voices. Even though machismo prevailed, photographs of marches are populated by forceful women. The excellent propaganda film *Salt of the Earth*, directed by Herbert J. Biberman with Rosaura Revueltas, which was released in 1958, is a suitable example. It is about the strike of miners in Grant County, New Mexico, in 1950. Plus, leaders like Dolores Huerta were instrumental in *el movimiento*.

Sor Juana Inés de La Cruz, the 17th-century Mexican nun whose poems and autobiographical writing are enormously influential in the Spanish-speaking world, was a role model for Chicanas. Indeed, her appeal continues unabated. Sor Juana defied the male ecclesiastical environment in Mexico to become the most important sonnetist of her time. Her confessor and other Catholic Church leaders repeatedly tried to quiet her, but she persisted in her struggle to bring attention to the plight of women, who in that period had very limited options in life: employment as a courtesan, marriage, prostitution, or the convent. Sor Juana, born out of wedlock, worked for the *Virreyna*, the Viceroy's wife, after which she moved to a convent. Her iconography was used in marches, rallies, and other protests.

### Is feminism a component of Chicanismo?

Some Chicanas like Anna Nieto-Gómez and Bernice Rincón fought the male-dominated society. They argued that within the struggle for labor improvement there was another equally important drive: for women to be seen as equal. They organized workshops, published newspapers and magazines, and spread the word widely. The by-product was an intellectual trend, *Xicanisma*, especially tangible in literature. It came about decades after *el movimiento* among authors too young to be part of it, like Gloria Anzaldúa, Ana Castillo, and Cherríe Moraga.

### Who was Dolores Huerta?

She was a cofounder of the National Farm Workers Association (NFWA) and an active leader in the Chicano movement. Huerta was born in Dawson, New Mexico, on April 10, 1930, and attended Stockton College in California. Fred Ross, who had such an influence on Cesar Chavez, also had a substantial impact on Huerta: he inspired her to seek ways to organize the Mexican American laborers at the local level. She and Chavez met through their work with the community service organization, which Ross founded.

Along with Chavez, she led marches, sit-ins, and boycotts. She was involved in the merging of the NFWA into the United Farm Workers (UFW), in which she served as part of the organization committee and lobbyist, negotiating contracts. Her work culminated in the landmark Agricultural Labor Relations Act of 1975 in California, a legislation protecting farm workers' rights to organize and bargain for their rights in the continental United States.

Huerta was also the UFW secretary-treasurer, and she established a foundation under her own name to advance the cause of Chicano workers, particularly of women. She served on the University of California Board of Regents, was inducted to the National Women's Hall of Fame, and was give the Eleanor Roosevelt Award from President Bill Clinton. Throughout her career as a nonviolence activist, she has been imprisoned approximately 20 times. Also, in 1988, while protesting a visit to San Francisco by the then vice president George H. W. Bush, she was beaten by a police officer with a nightstick. The attack was caught on tape. In a settlement, the San Francisco Police Department paid Huerta $850,000 and was forced to establish a stricter crowd-control policy.

## *What is the legacy of the Chicano Movement?*

Although often ignored in textbooks, the Chicano movement was an integral part of the civil rights era. Its immediate quest was to legitimize the rights of migrant laborers in the Southwest but, as it evolved, larger issues came into play: why have Mexican Americans been perceived as second-class citizens in the United States? Why didn't they have equal access to education, politics, and business opportunities? To what extent was their situation a legacy of the colonial period and the Treaty of Guadalupe Hidalgo? Initially, *el movimiento*, as it was called in Spanish, pertained to farm workers in Arizona, California, Colorado, and other states. But as marches attracted the nation's attention, other groups—students, service workers, and professionals—also joined in during the late 1960s and 1970s. A series of boycotts organized by Cesar Chavez ultimately brought the message to the entire population and people from all walks of life.

# 4

# YEARNING TO BREATHE FREE

### How is the word "immigration" defined?

The *Oxford English Dictionary* states that "it is the action of entering into a country for the purpose of settling in it." The definition conveys a sense of individual freedom. The settler arrives out of choice. Yet not all people in the United States trace their ancestry to an immigrant relative. Plus, the definition erases the line differentiating immigrants and settlers. Was William Bradford, who wrote about the Plymouth plantation, an immigrant? And what about Africans brought as slaves to the New World? American Indians were in these lands before the *Mayflower*. As a result of historical forces, they were forced to relocate to reservations specially defined by the US government.

### What are the meanings of "exile" and "refugee"?

These terms are different from "immigrant." Exiles are forced to leave their native country because of political reasons. A refugee departs because of natural reasons, although there are also cases where refugees have to leave because of an economic crisis.

Two more words to connect to this nomenclature are "expat," or a person living abroad for personal reasons, and "tourist," or a person who leaves temporarily for leisure. And then there are two more words: "settler," like those who lived in the Plymouth colony, and "slave," denoting someone taken in indenture from one place to another.

### Are all Latinos immigrants?

With the exception of those living in the southwestern territories before the Treaty of Guadalupe Hidalgo was signed, the majority of Latinos are descendants of immigrants. There are some who have come to the United States as exiles and refugees, and a few who arrived as tourists but remained.

By the way, immigrants often arrive through the legal door. However, from the 1980s onward, when the economies of Mexico and Central America were unstable, millions came without documents. They are often referred to as "illegals," or "illegal aliens."

### Is the term "illegal alien" derogatory?

Yes. Nobody is really illegal. The term is used as a noun, which means a person, not their actions, are illegal. In a speech, the Holocaust survivor and human-rights activist Elie Wiesel put it this way: "You who are called illegal aliens must know that no human being is illegal. That is a contradiction in terms. Human beings can be beautiful or more beautiful, they can be fat or skinny, they can be right or wrong, but illegal? How can a human being be illegal?" Latinos in general prefer to use "undocumented."

### What is the difference between an "immigrant" and a "migrant"?

An immigrant moves from one country to another. In that sense, the word "emigrant" denotes departure, whereas "immigrant" entails arrival. In contrast, a "migrant" moves within the same space. In that sense, Native Americans are migrants in the United States, having been relocated by the government a number of times in their history. So are Puerto Ricans. For sociologists, another way to describe this migration is as "internal immigration." And, in general, the United States population is quite mobile. That is, it tends to migrate, principally due to family, education, labor, and retirement.

### Isn't the United States a country of immigrants?

Always. The land was populated by aboriginal tribes, and the British settlers were the first immigrants.

In 1883, as Irish, Italian, and Jewish immigrants were arriving to American shores from Europe, Emma Lazarus, an English-speaking Sephardic Jew, wrote a sonnet that is engraved on the pedestal of the Statue of Liberty. Called "The New Colossus," it is a manifesto in favor of immigration, though of a particular kind: the poor—whom Lazarus describes as "the huddled masses yearning to breathe free." She advocates for opening the nation's doors to those in need. Her invitation isn't for the rich and educated. Needless to say, this approach is not always embodied in policy. Here is the poem:

Not like the brazen giant of Greek fame,
With conquering limbs astride from land to land;
Here at our sea-washed, sunset gates shall stand
A mighty woman with a torch, whose flame
Is the imprisoned lightning, and her name
Mother of Exiles. From her beacon-hand
Glows world-wide welcome; her mild eyes command
The air-bridged harbor that twin cities frame.
"Keep, ancient lands, your storied pomp!" cries she
With silent lips. "Give me your tired, your poor,
Your huddled masses yearning to breathe free,
The wretched refuse of your teeming shore.
Send these, the homeless, tempest-tost to me,
I lift my lamp beside the golden door!"

## How have the waves of immigration changed over time?

In general terms, prior to roughly 1950 the vast majority of immigrants to the United States were white and came from Europe by boat. After 1950, immigrants became far more diverse, arriving from Latin America, the Middle East, Asia, and Africa, and often by other means of transportation.

## Has the United States ever encouraged immigration from the Americas?

The notion of closed borders is new. Between the time of independence and the late 19th century, the country paid little attention to immigration. It was then when popular opinion began to shape around the number as well as economic and ethnic background of newcomers.

## Were there any laws regulating immigration before the late 19th century?

There were the Alien and Sedition Laws of the 18th century, but these didn't close the nation's borders. Such was the need of labor that during the American Civil War the flow of immigrants multiplied.

## Have laws been implemented to exclude a singular ethnic group?

The fear that dangerous people might be entering the country made Congress pass the Immigration Act of 1875, prohibiting criminals, convicts, and prostitutes from entering. This act also forbade "the immigration of any subject from China, Japan, or any Oriental country," because they were deemed undesirable. That approach was ratified in the Chinese Exclusion Act of 1882, in which Congress excluded only Chinese laborers and their wives already in the United States.

## When did Mexicans become the largest group within the Latino minority?

The process took about 50 years. It was at the beginning of the 20th century, with the Mexican Revolution, that large numbers of Mexicans moved to the United States to work in agriculture and the industrial sector. The reasons were multiple. The fall of the 30-year-long dictatorship of Porfirio Díaz, from 1881 to 1911, brought along violence, political turmoil, and labor uncertainty. But those decades were also a period of economic expansion in America. Seasonal workers sought to fill that need by moving north. In 1927, for instance, there were 63,700 Mexicans in the Midwest but the number increased during the summer to 80,000.

The need for a larger immigrant labor force increased during World War II, as soldiers left behind jobs to enlist in the Army. Their absence made it clear that America was suffering from a shortage of workers, and that an emergency program was needed.

## Since they are de facto US citizens, why should Puerto Ricans be considered immigrants?

It hasn't always been that way. Puerto Ricans became citizens with the Jones-Shafroth Act, a piece of legislation named after Congressman William A. Jones of Virginia, which was signed in 1917. The document left intact the island's colonial status but it affected its governing structure. It included a Bill of Rights and a 19-member Senate in Puerto Rico.

## What caused the Puerto Rican migration?

It was the result of the aftermath of the Spanish-American War, fought in 1898, in which Spain lost its satellites in the Caribbean Basin (Cuba, Puerto Rico) and in the Pacific (the Philippines and Guam). The United States intervened militarily three years earlier, but it was after the signing of the Treaty of Paris, bringing an end to the war, that the status of Puerto Ricans changed dramatically.

In the second half of the 19th century, Puerto Rican and Cuban political exiles lived in New York, Philadelphia, New Orleans, Tampa, and Key West, in settlements called *colonias*. Along with these, there were business ties, as sugar-related exports and tobacco connected the Caribbean with the United States. When tobacco shops and factories opened in Tampa and New York City, Puerto Rican and Cuban workers were employed to work in them. Plus, a group of separatists fighting for the independence of the Antilles—including José Martí, Ramón Emeterio Betances, Segundo Ruíz Belvis, Eugenio María de Hostos, Sotero Figueroa, Francisco "Pachín" Marín, and Lola Rodríguez de Tió occasionally made their headquarters in the northern and southern parts of the East Coast.

By the late 1910s, Puerto Rican migration to the United States intensified as the government in the island made it possible for mainland companies to hire agricultural and industrial workers from the island. A significant number were employed in New York City in the manufacturing and service industries.

### Who were the jíbaros?

*Jíbaro* is a Puerto Rican word used to describe an impoverished dweller from the island's countryside. After World War II, Puerto Rican communities in metropolises like New York City, Chicago, Newark, and Philadelphia grew. This wave is known as the Great Migration. Between 1940 and 1950 the number of Puerto Ricans in the mainland grew by 330.7%, and between 1950 and 1960 by 194.5%. To a large extent, *jíbaros* moved from agricultural jobs on the island to factories in urban environments in the United States.

### What was the reason for their migration?

The island underwent a process of industrialization, leaving the agricultural sector in bankruptcy. It began with what became known as Operation Bootstrap—in Spanish, *Operación Manos a la Obra*. In order to reduce unemployment, the Puerto Rican government promoted migration to the mainland. For decades after this mobilization, Puerto Rican culture was the lightning rod for Latinos in the Northeast. But by the 1980s, the Census Bureau began to register a stabilization and even diminution of this community and the explosion of other national groups within the Latino minority in the region, especially Mexicans and Central Americans (Salvadorans, Guatemalans, Nicaraguans, etc.).

### When did Puerto Ricans first settle in New York?

The first settlers arrived in the late 19th century. They were mostly *tabaqueros*, or cigar workers. They were known as the educated segment of the working class. There were also munitions factories employing Puerto Ricans. The diaspora increased after the Spanish-American War. Bernardo Vega, a *tabaquero* activist born in 1885, described the urban landscape in his *Memoirs*. His book is an invaluable resource for understanding the circumstance of Puerto Ricans and their connection with Tammany Hall. Another important early figure, also interested in politics, was Jesús Colón, author of *A Puerto Rican in New York and Other Sketches*.

The community increased after the Depression, when the arrival of *jíbaros* reconfigured it. By the end of World War II, New York had the largest concentration of Puerto Ricans outside San Juan. (Philadelphia, Chicago, and Newark followed closely.) That tide, which took place by airplane, is known as the Great Migration. It was also the time of Operation Bootstrap. This resulted in an emergence of a fresh culture in the United States. The list of artists connected with New York

City is enormous, from Tito Puente to Marc Anthony. Julia de Burgos wrote about it in *Canción de la verdad sencilla* (1939), as did Pedro Pietri, in *Puerto Rican Obituary* (1971).

### What is the Loisaida?

The term was coined in the 1970s by the activists Chino García and Bimbo Rivas to refer to the area of Manhattan where Puerto Ricans lived predominantly. It is a Spanglish variation of the name Lower East Side, an area from east of Avenue A bounded by 14th Street, Houston Street, and the East River.

This was a region populated by Jewish immigrants at the end of the 20th century and prior to them by Irish newcomers. The photographer Jacob Riis depicted it in his provocative book *How the Other Half Lives* (1890), in which he portrayed the disastrous living conditions of the working class.

Puerto Ricans originally settled in East Harlem, North Brooklyn, the South Bronx, and *La Loisaida*. The Harlem section came to be known as *El Barrio*. Literary representations of it include Piri Thomas's *Down These Mean Streets* (1967) and Edward Rivera's *Family Installments* (1982). The term "Nuyorrican" refers to a type of double consciousness, one defined by identities in transition, in hybrid stage.

### Why are Puerto Ricans perceived by other Latinos as unique?

They are US passport carriers. Also, their American citizenship makes them eligible for a series of government programs, including welfare. They are seen as neither refugees nor immigrants.

### Where is Vieques?

It is an island, also known as Isla Nena, off of Puerto Rico's east coast. It became a municipality of Puerto Rico in 1843 but the American government, after the Spanish-American War, used it as a strategic site to engage in military practice. It has been a sore point for Puerto Ricans as it signified the US dominance of the island. Protests have been staged to push out the US army.

### Has there been another wave of Puerto Rican migration?

Yes. In 2014, a financial crisis in the island, mainly a result of debt owned by the government and inept politicians, resulted in a precarious economy and a default on a bond of $58 million. The crisis caused an enormous amount of job losses and an exodus of Puerto Ricans to the mainland United States. Unlike all prior crises, this one predominantly caused a relocation of upper-class and middle-class people, who moved to Florida, California, and states in the Midwest.

### Where does the word "Caribbean" come from?

The etymology comes from Carib, a West Indian tribe. They apparently moved from the Orinoco rainforest in Venezuela to the Caribbean archipelago and were known in Europe for their violent, combative character. Several of their words, like "hurricane," have become part of the English language. Shakespeare never left England, yet his play *The Tempest* (1611), about a ruler called Prospero and two opposing characters, the spiritual Ariel and the brutish Caliban (the latter a clear reference to his origins), could have been inspired by the tribe.

### What kind of immigration took place after Fidel Castro's 1958–1959 revolution?

During the first three years of Castro's regime, the middle and upper classes stampeded out of the island. The diaspora relocated to Puerto Rico, Mexico, Spain, Germany, the Nordic countries, but especially in the United States. Florida and New Jersey in particular became Cuban safe havens. This departure wasn't only about ideology and economics.

The Communist regime forbade free enterprise but also freedom of religion. In the end, whites were highly represented among the exiles. The result was a darkening of Cuba's population.

It is important to remember that exile has been a fixture of Hispanic life since the 15th century. The forced conversion and expulsion of the Jewish and Muslim populations from the Iberian Peninsula constitute "an unwilling absence from one's own country or home," which is the standard definition of exile. That absence might be caused by ethnic, political, and religious factors. For example, Domingo Faustino Sarmiento, an Argentine intellectual known for the canonical work *Facundo: or, Civilization and Barbarism* (1845), and the future president of his country, lived in Chile to escape the tyrannical regime of Juan Manuel de Rosas. Cubans themselves had experienced other exiles in the past. José Martí was forced out of the island and lived in Key West, Florida, and New York, among other places.

### How did the Cuban émigrés assimilate to the American way of life?

As Cuban émigrés entered the United States as political refugees, they were eligible to receive government benefits (education, health care, and so on) that other Latinos don't enjoy. The first generation of exiles after the revolution was mostly educated. Their first years were spent waiting for Castro's power to implode. When that didn't happen, they began to assimilate to the United States, soon becoming business executives, political leaders, journalists, teachers, and other professionals.

### What kind of relationship does the exile community have with Havana?

This is a tense relationship defined by anger and frustration. The exiles in Miami are known in Cuba as *gusanos*, or worms. They are portrayed as C.I.A. operatives eager to unsettle Castro's government. In turn, the Cuban exiles accuse the Communist regime of abuse of power, corruption, intimidation, and torture. Sometimes members of the same family, separated by an abysmal nine miles, are the protagonists of this animosity.

### What was Operation Peter Pan about?

With Castro's ascent to power in Havana, upper- and middle-class parents feared for the future of their children. They made an effort to secretly send them to the United States on a temporary basis. Starting on December 26, 1960, some 14,000 unaccompanied children, between the ages of 6 and 18, were part of the exodus. In Spanish, the effort was known as *Operación Pedro Pan*, a reference to the children's literature character prematurely forced into adulthood.

The program highlighted the tension between Cuba and the American government. It was seen by Castro's regime as a psychological strategy. Approximately 6,000 children ended up in the care of friends and relatives while the remaining 8,000 were under the care of the federal government. Harrowing stories of separation, nostalgia, and reunion were a fixture of the Cuban American community.

### What is the Mariel Boatlift?

In 1980 a public protest took place in Havana when at first dozens, then hundreds of people occupied the Peruvian embassy protesting Castro's curtailing of individual freedom. Soon the protest became a diplomatic crisis of international proportions. Images of the standoff were broadcast on TV constantly. Eventually, Fidel Castro, *el líder máximo*, allowed the mob to leave the island in boats. But he also emptied the country's jails, sending criminals into exile. That generation of Cuban exiles is known as *marielitos*.

## What is a balsero?

The word means *rafter* in Spanish. In their desire to escape repression, Cubans sought any available alternative to leave the island, including building makeshift boats out of empty oil drums, truck tires, wood, and any other floating object. Miami is 90 miles away from Cuba. At night one is able to see the lights across the ocean. The outpouring of *balseros* varied, according to security and the weather. According to some estimates, approximately 17,000 *balseros* had arrived in the United States from Cuba by 1994.

## What was the Elián Gonzáles affair about?

A victim of the *balsero* rift, Gonzáles was a five-year-old boy who left the island, along with his mother, Elisabet Brotons, to come to the United States. Elián's father, from whom his mother was divorced, remained in Cuba. Elián's mother drowned at sea, and the child was found floating in the ocean off the coast of Florida on Thanksgiving Day 1998. His rescue became an international case as relatives who took guardianship of Elián blamed Fidel Castro's regime for generating the kind of poverty and repression that resulted in *balseros* risking their lives. The father, supported by the Cuban government, demanded that the boy be returned. The Cuban exile community declared that they would never willingly return Elián. At the same time, a majority of non-Cuban Latinos sided with the American mainstream in their support of the child's return to his father. Eventually, US Attorney General Janet Reno ordered federal officers to break into the relative's house on April 22, 1999, and take the boy away. He was returned to his father, with whom he stayed for some time in the United States. They returned to Cuba in June of that year.

## What about the Dominican Republic?

It shares a border with Haiti and, together, the two form the island once called Hispaniola, where Columbus first settled.

The roots of the Dominican American community date back at least to 1844, when the Dominican Republic achieved its independence from Spain. Soon after, President Ulysses S. Grant attempted to annex it, just as the United States had done with Puerto Rico and, to some extent, Cuba, but he encountered opposition from various senators. In 1905 it became a protectorate of the United States, which ruled over it through a military regime between 1916 and 1924. In short, the political, economic, and cultural facets of the island have always been dependent on American interests.

### What caused the flight of immigrants from the Dominican Republic?

Rafael Leónidas Trujillo, whose dictatorship lasted from 1930 to 1961, was a fervent anti-Communist who sided with the Allies during World War II. He was one of the only Latin American leaders who opened up national borders to Jewish refugees from Eastern Europe in the 1930s. The effort was in tune with his policy of "whitening" the population of the Dominican Republic. In 1937, he ordered the massacre of 20,000 dark-skinned Haitians. On the other hand, he was instrumental in the modernization of his country, allowing the middle class to steadily grow and, in general, improving the economic situation, particularly in the agricultural sector. He was also repressive and destroyed his enemies, as was the case of the Mirabal sisters, chronicled in Julia Alvarez's novel *In the Time of the Butterflies* (1994). It was after his regime was overthrown that the Dominican Republic entered a period of recession and unemployment that brought people out.

### Where is the Dominican American community based?

They are mostly concentrated in New York, especially the neighborhood of Washington Heights. The vast majority of Dominican Americans are of a mix of African slaves and aboriginal ancestry. The second and third generations retain a strong loyalty toward their island of origin. As is the case for Puerto Ricans living in the United States, Dominican American culture is shaped by the interplay between island and US-born Dominican American culture. At times this mixing erases the line between the native and diasporic. Aside from Alvarez, the community has produced intellectuals, performance artists, and scholars like Pedro Henríquez Ureña, Silvio Torres-Saillant, Josefina Báez, Daisy Cocco De Filippis, and Frank Gutiérrez.

### Has immigration from Spanish-speaking countries always been incessant?

Economic insecurity and political repression in Latin America are the central factors in the massive northbound movement of people across the hemisphere. Ever since newly formed republics like Mexico, Argentina, Colombia, Venezuela, and Peru fought against Spain to achieve their independence, their path to stability has been filled with landmines. Only in the late 20th century did democracy become a pattern in most of them and even then it hasn't been free of threats. Spanish-speaking immigrants to the United States have run away from repressive regimes and uncertain labor conditions. Their arrival, legal and otherwise, has been ongoing since the 1920s. Different groups have arrived at different periods, depending on the national juncture. The largest portion of Spanish-speaking immigrants at the dawn of the late 19th century was from Puerto Rico.

### What is the apex of Central American immigration?

The civil wars in Guatemala, El Salvador, and Nicaragua in the 1980s forced people to emigrate. The United States became a favorite target. Depending on the country of origin—from

Honduras and Costa Rica to Panama—the journey included a passage through various borders.

## What kinds of wars?

Political instability began in Guatemala in 1944 and continued until the 1970s. The nation's population, divided into Mayans and mestizos, each using a different language and living in different parts of the country, was in turmoil as a result of repeated coup d'états as well as social and economic divisions. A 36-year-long civil war started in 1970. It would ultimately claim 200,000 victims. It was during the dictatorial regime of Efraín Ríos Montt, in 1982–1983, that most people left—500,000, according to some estimates. (The country had a total population of more than 10 million.) Most Guatemalan Americans today retain connections with the homeland.

In El Salvador, economic malaise and political repression prompted a rebellion, with the goal of attaining improvement for large numbers of the poor. (Eventually the dollar was adopted as the nation's currency.) A civil war took place between 1980 and 1992 in which it is estimated that 75,000 people were killed. Running away from the strife, thousands left the country. By the middle of the 1980s, it was estimated that approximately 850,000 Salvadorans lived in the United States. Their immigration had been minimal before the war.

The United States has used Nicaragua as a playing field for foreign policy since the early 20th century, in large part because the two countries share a passage—the Nicaragua Canal—joining the Atlantic and Pacific Oceans. In 1912 US marines invaded the country. Augusto Cesar Sandino emerged as a leading figure of the opposition but was assassinated; instead a corrupt dictatorship, led by Anastasio Somoza and his sons, Luis and Anastasio Jr., prevailed. In the 1970s the Sandinista National Liberation Front emerged as an alternative force for the poor and disenchanted. After violent confrontations, the

Sandinistas defeated the dictatorship in 1979. The United States sought to bring the Front down in what became the Iran-Contra Affair.

### What was the Iran-Contra Affair about?

After the Iran hostage crisis in the early 1980s, within President Ronald Reagan's cabinet an effort was made to orchestrate a counterrevolution against the Sandinista government of Daniel Ortega in Nicaragua. The money for weapons came from Middle Eastern sources and it went to support a group called the "Contras," designed to undermine the Sandinistas. Because Congress didn't approve funds for the rebellion, when the channeling of money from other government sources became known it was quickly deemed illegal. This revelation became a scandal in the United States that almost brought down Reagan's presidency. The civil war in Nicaragua resulted in a massive northbound movement of people seeking refuge. This migration took place over several years and itself became a subject of controversy. Nicaraguans in the United States were allowed to apply for political asylum, given their status as refugees. A strong community developed, especially in Miami.

### How about immigration from South America to the United States?

Because the region is not as geographically close to the United States, it has not been much of a target for American intervention. However, from Colombia to Uruguay, economic debacles and political strife have resulted in an exodus that, again, found its magnet north of the Rio Grande. This is not to say that the United States has not supported coups and repressive governments in the region. In 1973—on September 11—Augusto Pinochet, a Chilean general backed by the United States, orchestrated an insurrection against the elected president Salvador Allende, pushing Allende to commit suicide, and then started a dictatorship.

At one point in the 1990s the Census Bureau added a category of Latinos called "Central and South Americans." It included people from Chile, Ecuador, Peru, and Paraguay. The category was eventually eliminated. In any event, counted together, there were more South Americans in the United States in 2014, 2,856,000, than Cubans. The country where the largest number of immigrants came from was Colombia with 707,000, followed by Peru with 449,000, and Ecuador with 424,000.

### Why has Colombia been a source of immigration?

The exodus from Colombia toward the United States was the result of violence, economic instability, and the cartels that turned Colombia into a major provider of drugs—*el narcotráfico*—in the Western Hemisphere. People from all backgrounds have moved north, not only from metropolitan centers like Bogotá and Medellín but from rural areas too. They have mostly settled in Florida, but also in New York, New Jersey, and Texas.

### And Venezuela: in what way have people from there been drawn to the United States?

In 2014 there were 216,000 Venezuelan immigrants in the United States. Venezuela was a relatively stable country until the 1980s, when an economic crisis brought along unemployment and people began to look for ways of escape. There was inflation, currency devaluation, coup d'états, and presidential impeachment, and, eventually, the election of a leftist leader, Hugo Chávez. Chávez aligned with Fidel Castro's policies, fashioning himself as a hemispheric leader seeking to galvanize the resentment against, and opposition to, the United States for decades of abuse of power in Latin America. Chávez's rhetoric found its target in President George W. Bush, an unpopular figure worldwide because of his decision to invade Iraq and bring down the dictatorship of Saddam Hussein, whom he claimed was building weapons of mass destruction. In speech after speech, Chávez turned himself into a kind of Robin Hood of the poor nations, eager to fight the rich. His power depended not only on words but on Venezuela's considerable oil resources. The country is a main provider to several neighbors, from Brazil to Argentina. It also used to sell crude to the United States.

Chávez died in 2013 at the age of 59. His hand-picked successor was Nicolás Maduro, a former bus driver loyal to Chávez but with little political experience. His reign was marked by egregious mismanagement of the economy, widespread scarcity of goods in the nation's supermarkets, and heightened ideological tension with the United States. Venezuelans tried to leave in hordes. Nearby countries like Colombia, Panama, Peru, and Chile became magnets of immigration. And in the Dominican Republic, the size of the Venezuelan community quadrupled in only a few years.

Middle-class Venezuelans immigrated to the United States in the 1990s. Their favorite destinations became Florida, New York, Texas, New Jersey, and California. After Chávez's death, the exodus also included people from lower-income brackets.

### Are Brazilians considered Latinos?

The conquest of the Americas wasn't carried out by Spain alone. Portugal was another major colonial empire in the 16th century. And the French and Dutch also took a role in exploring the New World. Each left an imprint on their colonies.

Brazil, which stands as the largest country in South America, not only geographically but in demographic terms too, adopted an idiosyncratic Portuguese as its language. In 2014, the Brazilian population was 207,847,528, while the number of Brazilian immigrants in the United States numbered

336,000—in other words, about 1.6% of that country's population. Brazil has traditionally been seen as something of an island within the South American continent. The Dominican writer Pedro Henríquez Ureña campaigned to debunk the term *América latina*, claiming it was misleading. Instead, he suggested the proper term for Latin America would be an amalgam of Hispanic and Luso (e.g., Portuguese) Americas, or *la América hispánica y la América portuguesa*, stressing the linguistic and cultural uniqueness of the continent's colonial pasts. As a result of their distinctiveness, Brazilians are and are not part of the minority. That distinctiveness is evident in their colorful style and contagious music, from samba to bossa nova. Issues of race are approached in Brazil with an openness unmatched in other parts of the region. The country was a target of the Portuguese slave trade, and thus blacks were brought there in large numbers.

### Where have Brazilians settled in the United States?

Primarily in Florida, Massachusetts, California, New York, and New Jersey. There is a "Little Brazil" near 46th Street in Manhattan. Immigrants are from all walks of life: black and white, working class and well-to-do, male and female.

### What brought along the Brazilian immigration?

Brazil used to be known as a target, not a source, of immigration. Jews, Germans, Italians, Japanese, and other national groups arrived at various points before the mid-20th century. The reversal started with the Gétulio Vargas dictatorship, which lasted from 1930 to 1945 and from 1951 until his suicide in 1954. During this period the labor force migrated to industrial nations when needed, including the United States.

A decade after Vargas's suicide, another coup d'état brought a new military regime to Brazil that lasted until 1985. The period was marked by what became known as "the Brazilian miracle," a sense that the nation's economy was destined to be a major player in world affairs. But a series of mismanaged financial decisions brought along inflation, which in turn created a stagnant financial market. Finally, in 1984 a presidential election took place in which opposition civilian candidates won.

The United States has been the home—temporary and permanent—of intellectuals, politicians, and artists. Such figures have included Carmen Miranda, Cândido Portinari, Antonio Carlos Jobim, and Juscelino Kubitschek.

### What were living conditions like for Mexican immigrants in the United States during the 20th century?

After World War II, the living and labor conditions of Mexican Americans in the Southwest were depressed. Xenophobia and racism played a role in keeping Spanish-speaking people in low-entry jobs. The Latino middle class was small and, in general, disconnected from the grass roots. The poor lived in ghettos in major urban centers on both coasts of the country, including East L.A. in California and Spanish Harlem in New York.

### What does bracero mean?

In Spanish bracero refers to a legally contracted worker. The program ran from August 4, 1942, to December 31, 1964. It was a formal binational agreement between the governments that allowed the United States to import labor from Mexico. In those 22 years a total of five million Mexican workers entered, and settled, in 24 different states of the nation. Many of those workers were employed in the railroad industry.

The provisions of the program were clear-cut: braceros were provided free housing and sanitary labor conditions; they were paid at least the equivalent to what American citizens received for the same job and not less than 30 cents an hour; they were guaranteed employment for three months of the contract period and a subsistence wage of $3 in case they lost their job; and they were guaranteed round-trip transportation from and to Mexico.

### Was the program well received nationwide?

It was controversial to say the least. There were those who argued that American domestic workers were being impacted by it. Others believed that illegal workers were taking advantage of the system to infiltrate the country. In response, the Eisenhower administration started Operation Wetback, a program to deport illegal Mexicans back to their native country. The program was supported by Attorney General Herbert Brownell.

### How many people were deported during Operation Wetback?

According to the Immigration and Naturalization Service, some 1.3 million people were sent back to Mexico, but the exact number is impossible to know.

### Have most undocumented immigrants come from Mexico?

The majority of undocumented immigrants from the 1980s onward were from Mexico and Central America. The civil wars in Guatemala, El Salvador, and Nicaragua forced people to seek better opportunities in *El Norte*. By 2015, about half of all undocumented immigrants were from Mexico. The other half was from Central America.

### Who are the DREAMers?

The DREAM Act comes from the acronym for Development, Relief, and Education for Alien Minors. It was introduced as legislation in 2001 by US senators Dick Durbin and Orrin

Hatch. The DREAMers are the children of undocumented immigrants who crossed the border from the 1980s onward. These minors were either born or raised in the United States and are not considered accountable for the decisions to immigrate made by their parents. The DREAM Act proposes an amnesty to those who are law-abiding citizens and have not committed a crime.

### Did the DREAM Act pass?

It never did. It was caught in ideological battles between liberals and conservatives. These battles were exacerbated during the Obama administration. Donald Trump campaigned in 2016 with the message that undocumented aliens—he repeatedly called them "illegals"—needed to be deported back to Mexico.

### Why deport undocumented immigrants to Mexico if half of them come from other countries?

Trump frequently uses "Mexico" as a metonym to refer to all Latinos. He once purportedly said that "Puerto Ricans are the worst Mexicans."

### Was Donald Trump the first US president to deport undocumented immigrants?

No, George W. Bush was the first, although the number of deported people was small in comparison to the number sent back during the Obama administration. The latter administration deported close to 3 million, up 23% from the Bush years.

### Was there legislation to counteract this massive movement?

The 1986 Immigration Reform and Control Act was designed to stop it. Among other strategies, it required employers to ask laborers for proof of citizenship. It also legalized noncitizens who met certain criteria, so it was a de facto amnesty program. This act was amended in 1990, giving preference to workers who were professionals with advanced degrees.

### Is deportation legal?

It depends on the moment in history one refers to. The Chinese Exclusion Act of 1882 was evidently designed to eliminate the undesirables through deportation. And the Illegal Immigration Reform and Immigrant Responsibility Act of 1996, brought in to reinforce the legislation passed in 1952, allowed law enforcement to deport or exclude a person without a formal hearing. This allowed for the deportation of large numbers of people crossing the border.

### What about the mass protests of 2006?

After the terrorist attacks against the World Trade Center on September 11, 2001, the government declared war on Al-Qaeda, the organization responsible for orchestrating the attacks. That war materialized first in Afghanistan against the Taliban regime in power, then in Iraq against the dictatorship of Saddam Hussein. Simultaneously, the nation's geographic borders attracted much attention. Could another attack take place inside the United States? What efforts could be implemented to stop potential terrorists from infiltrating the country?

At the same time, dramatic ethnic changes became evident as the Census Bureau declared, in 2002, that the Latino minority, ahead of all expectations, was already the largest in the country, with Spanish the second most frequently used language. Conservative groups reacted with unease. On the one hand, the nation was visibly under threat from the outside; on the other, it was undergoing an internal turmoil with an equally difficult outcome. Were Latinos learning English at the same speed as previous immigrants? Was the United States about to be divided along ethnic, cultural, and linguistic lines?

As Congress and the Senate debated immigration reforms, including a guest-worker program that would be a form of amnesty, the toughening of border patrols, and the building of a wall along the US-Mexico border, people of different persuasions took to the street to let their views be known. From Los Angeles to Dallas and Washington DC, supporters of a lax approach to immigration marched while opponents to any type of amnesty manifested themselves in newspapers and on TV and in other media.

### Since when did the US-Mexico border become a nation unto its own?

The transformation started after World War II. The border extends from southern California through central Arizona and New Mexico, to Texas and the Gulf of Mexico. On the other side, it connects the states of Baja California, Sonora, Chihuahua, Coahuila, Nuevo León, and Tamaulipas. It has a length of 2,000 miles. Its present form was established in 1848, after the Mexican-American War ended and the Treaty of Guadalupe Hidalgo and the Gadsden Purchase were signed. It brings together—or apart, depending on how one sees it— two dramatically different civilizations: the English-speaking Anglo to the north, and the Spanish-speaking Hispanic to the south.

Throughout history, the border has been extraordinarily porous. The United States has gone from welcoming *braceros* and other crossers to blocking their passage through a specially trained patrolling force. This force has at times been supported by vigilantes and other volunteers. The passage runs in more than one way: people running away from the law and from financial problems cross from north to south too.

There are approximately 25 million people living in and around the region. Sweatshops, known as *maquiladoras*, employ workers, particularly young women, in the manufacturing of inexpensive items designed for export. A global economy has forced countries like Mexico to create these types of industrial growths.

Depending on the location, the language spoken along the US-Mexico border might range from English to Spanish and—more consistently—Spanglish.

### When was the US Border Patrol formed?

It was established in 1924 to police the US-Mexican border. Its purpose was to limit newcomers perceived to be potential "public charges," that is, welfare users.

### Has the rationale for exclusion always used nationality?

Not at all. Among the most significant is the Immigration Act of 1924, known for introducing a literacy test. This is also the act that famously refused entry for "all idiots, imbeciles, feeble-minded persons, epileptics, insane persons; persons who have had one or more attacks of insanity at any time previously; persons of constitutional psychopathic inferiority; persons with chronic alcoholism; persons afflicted with tuberculosis of any form or with loathsome or dangerous contagious diseases; persons not comprehended within any of the foregoing excluded classes who are found to be and are certified by the examining surgeon as being mentally or physically defective, such physical defect being of a nature which may affect the ability of such alien to earn a living." The test established by the act served as a filter. Mexican laborers able to enter the United States before 1917 were no longer accepted because they failed the test.

### What other acts followed?

The National Origins Act of 1921, designed as a response to post–World War I immigration, was the first to establish quotas. It was legislated and approved by Congress three years later. Then the 1952 Immigration and Nationality Act, a preferential system, was established in reaction to the onslaught of refugees after World War II. Congress allocated the first 50% of the quota to skilled immigrants and the second to relatives of citizens and persons already in the United States.

Then came the 1965 Immigration Nationality Act, which eliminated restrictions on Asian immigrants. It also announced specific numbers: a limit of 120,000 newcomers from the Western Hemisphere was set, with no country exceeding 20,000. This act also emphasized family connections, giving preference to people with established ties to Americans.

### Are anti-Trump protests connected to his views on deportation?

Yes. During his presidential campaign, he repeatedly stated that one of his priorities was to build a wall between Mexico and the United States and have Mexico pay for it. This infuriated large numbers of people who saw the approach as a refutation of globalism. Of course, Trump is against international trade. He is a pragmatic populist and an antiglobalist. He has offered to create millions of jobs to compensate for those that have been lost to trade agreements with China and Mexico. Trump sees the deserving beneficiaries of those jobs as, for the most part, white Americans who didn't benefit from global trade agreements made over the last few decades of the 20th century.

### Is Trump anti-immigrants and anti-Latino?

It is hard to say what Trump's views are. It is also difficult to assess if he is a Hispanophobe, although at times it appears that way.

### Have Latino immigrants prospered in the United States?

No doubt, although entrance to the middle class has been slow. The number of small businesses in barrios all across the nation has multiplied exponentially, at three times the national average, in the 21st century.

### What is the overall position of Latinos on immigration?

More than 75% of Latino families include at least one recent immigrant (and sometimes more). Overall, judging by educational, media, and other manifestations, it is obvious that patriotism—love for, and gratitude to, the United States—is a strong collective emotion. It would be a mistake to suggest that all Latinos are supportive of a more lenient policy toward immigration. As is the case of Americans in general, there is a solid number of Latinos eager to tighten the US-Mexico border. This was clear before and on March 1, 2006, when a series of national marches, from Los Angeles to Dallas, and from Chicago to Boston, took place. These marches were largely constituted by Latinos and other ethnic Americans who opposed a proposal, debated in the Senate and Congress, to, among other things, create a guest-worker program, offer amnesty to some illegal residents in the United States for some years, and build a wall on the border.

### Is the issue of immigration linked to national security?

In the aftermath of the tragic events of September 11, 2001, where scores of legal and undocumented workers died, along with thousands of other Americans, in the World Trade Center, the Pentagon, and onboard the commercial flights piloted by terrorists, the issue of security became politically charged. Even though there were instances of attempted terrorists infiltrating the United States from Canada, the US-Mexico border was seen as more porous. As security was emphasized, the question of who is allowed into the country became relevant. Thus, immigration was at the center of the nation's political radar.

# 5

# FAMILY SECRETS

*Is* la familia, *the Latino family, closely knit?*

Yes, members of the Latino family tend to see themselves as a nucleus of support. While Latino families adhere to traditional principles, the truth is that there are important differences within the culture, defined across national, ethnic, geographical, and economic lines. In the view of sociologists, agricultural families tend to be more traditional, whereas urban families are considered to be more transitional. Also, the families of newly arrived immigrants tend to embrace different values from families whose US roots date back at least a couple of generations. The difference might be measured through the connection with the place once called home. Recent immigrants, for instance, tend to be more superstitious than second-generation Latinos. They also see politicians and the overall political process with more suspicion. And they are less inclined to establish solid relationships with people of other races. All this changes as the process of assimilation gets under way across generations.

*In what way is that concept related to history?*

The conquistadors, explorers, and missionaries from the Iberian Peninsula who made the journey across the Atlantic Ocean were coming from a feudal system that valued loyalty and bravery. They were predominantly men—the principal geographical source of conquistadors was the region of Extremadura—who left their wives and children at home. Their devotion to the Catholic kings and their devout faith in the Church defined their psychological motives. They were unlike the colonists of the *Mayflower*, who defined themselves as children of a new Canaan, running away from intolerance and religious persecution and eager to settle as far away as possible from the motherland—yet eager to upstage that motherland in their colonial quest. In other words, the conquistadors nurtured neither nationalist nor entrepreneurial dreams. Instead, their mission was to turn the Americas into the Spanish Crown's ideological and financial satellites.

### Are there racial tensions among Latinos?

Indeed, there are, and *la familia* is frequently a microcosm for them. One is able to see them tangibly in memoirs such as Piri Thomas's *Down These Mean Streets* and Edward Rivera's *Family Installments*. As a consequence of historical events, Latinos of white, European descent retain a leading role in the racial hierarchy, whereas there is unquestionable racism toward aboriginal and black Latinos, not only by white Latinos but by nonwhites as well. In other words, Latino racism is a strong feeling of intra-ethnic emotion. After the arrival of the Spaniards to the New World, there was a heated discussion among theologians and other thinkers in Spain and elsewhere in Europe about the "humanity" of the native population. Should they be seen as equals to Europeans? Opinions were divided. Spaniards depicted the ways in which Indians dressed, ate, bred and educated their infants, and engaged in warfare as awkward. Theologians used biblical references to suggest that the Indians were closer to chimpanzees than to humans. Their effort at evangelizing the Indians was about "civilizing" them, meaning making them accept the Christian faith and therefore allowing them the means to become fully human. They took the same stance toward their slaves, whom the Europeans considered even less human.

During the colonial period in Latin America, there was a strict racial structure that put Spaniards at the top, followed by criollos (Spaniards born in the Americas), mestizos, indigenous people, blacks, and other by-products of miscegenation, such as mulattos (a person of white and black ancestry) and *sambos* (black or indigenous with European blood). This racial tension extends to the larger world. Latinos of different ethnic backgrounds tend to live separately from each other. Likewise, Latino political figures tend to be either European or mestizo.

### How did blacks come to the New World?

Blacks were brought to the Americas as slaves through the slave trade from Africa in the 16th century. In response, a handful of progressive priests who were witnesses of the colonization effort accused explorers, missionaries, and other Europeans in the Americas of abusing the aboriginals. One of the most celebrated promoters of this view was Fray Bartolomé de Las Casas, known for the so-called *leyenda negra*, the black legend. In works like *A Short Account of the Destruction of the Indies* (1552), he showed that what the Iberian colonialists were engaged in was genocide. He denounced their abuses and struggled to convince his readership in the Old World of the dignity of the aboriginal population.

### What is a mestizo?

Latinos are a multiethnic people. In the Caribbean, the African racial influence is strong, so Cubans, Dominicans, and Puerto Ricans in the United States, as well as Venezuelans, Panamanians, and others from the larger Antillean constellation, retain this ancestry. The indigenous heritage is visible in the region too. (The Tainos were the first inhabitants of Borinquen, as Puerto Rico was called.) In Mexico and the various countries of Central America, the aboriginal heritage looms larger. The encounter between Europeans and the indigenous population during the colonial period resulted in a new racial category known as *mestizaje*.

During the colonial period, a racial hierarchy evolved. Spaniards sat at the top, Creoles came second, with mestizos in third place, Indians in fourth, and blacks at the bottom. This hierarchy manifested itself in politics, business and education and in every other level of society. Mexico's independence later pushed Creoles to the top and expanded the power of mestizos. When the Treaty of Guadalupe Hidalgo and the Gadsden Purchase were concluded, the United States inherited the populations of the southwestern states. Although the treaty promised a fair and equal treatment to everyone, Mexicans, especially those of mixed race, just like Indians, were not considered citizens. In 1849 states like California, New Mexico, and Arizona limited citizenship to whites.

### How do Latinos perceive their indigenous past today?

There has always been ambivalence among people in the Americas—and, by extension, among Latinos—toward the region's indigenous past. Should one look to Europe to understand the roots of the United States? Or should the Indian past serve as the original model? Periodically there are movements to reclaim the aboriginal past. There are also attempts to turn *mestizaje* into a philosophy. José Vasconcelos, a Mexican thinker and politician, published his treatise *The Cosmic Race* (1927), in which he discussed a synthesis of races and suggested that mestizos were called to dominate the earth in the 21st century. The volume became a manifesto of sorts for students involved in the Chicano movement of the 1960s. It has regained currency as the Trump administration has given room to nativist views of America.

### In what sense are mestizaje and Afro-Latin identity different?

As a term, *mestizaje* is embraced in Mexico and Central America. It is well known elsewhere although it doesn't retain the same gravitas. There are toponymic differences as well: for instance, in Guatemala mestizos are called *ladinos*.

Afro-Latin identity is connected with the Caribbean Basin, Brazil, Venezuela, the eastern side of Colombia, Panama, and other countries in the region. This is the region that was targeted by the slave trade and, thus, the African influence is more pronounced in these areas. This is seen at multiple levels, from religion to politics and beyond.

As a result of transculturation, Catholicism is at the core of all Latin American—and, therefore, Latino—ways of life. Yet the nuances between *mestizaje* and Afro-Latin cultures are enormous, always based on the ethnic elements present at a specific location.

### Will there ever be a postracial Latinidad?

To me it is impossible to imagine such a state. *Latinidad*, as such, is a hodgepodge. It is not the negation of its various components but its summation. On the surface, *Latinidad* is a continuum. It thrives through subtle intra-ethnic connections. Yet it would be foolish not to acknowledge the conflict that exists at its core. After all, this collective identity is the result of centuries of accrued tension.

### Returning to la familia, what are its different roles?

These roles are best understood through religious iconography. In Hispanic Catholicism, the mother is fundamental. In Mexico, the Virgin of Guadalupe is the most important figure, surpassing even Jesus Christ. Likewise, the millions of Mexican Americans in the United States consider themselves *guadalupanos*. The same ought to be said about the Caribbean Basin, where a myriad of motherly icons, such as la Virgen de la Caridad del Cobre, also take a predominant role. These figures embrace the concept of *marianismo* and are perceived as protectors and enablers.

### What vision of manhood did the conquistadors bring along?

Their machismo—their manhood—was an essential component of their character. Without their spouses, they felt free to take advantage of the aboriginal female population. The result was a rapid increase of offspring from Iberian fathers and Indian mothers, that is, the birth of the mestizo civilization. Needless to say, the Spanish conquistadors seldom acknowledged their offspring in the Americas, leaving the mothers alone and without support. Hernán Cortés, the representative leader of the defeat of the Aztec Empire, left behind an abundant progeny, both white and mestizo. His mistress, Doña Marina, known in Mexico as La Malinche, served him not only as lover and confidant but as translator and strategist. In Mexico, the word *malinchista* is used to refer to both an antipatriotic person or a traitor to one's country.

### What is machismo?

The stereotype of the macho is not exclusive to Hispanic society. It is pervasive all across the Mediterranean civilizations, from Portugal to Italy, from Spain to Greece. It projected itself onto the Americas through conquest and colonization. It represents men as aggressive, domineering, and self-confident. It depicts men as strong, in contrast with the weakness of women. Machismo is a cultural trait. Its representations are ever present in movies, TV, literature, and art.

### What about marianismo?

*Marianismo* is a philosophy of female self-sacrifice. It might well be seen as the reverse side of machismo. It is rooted in Iberian

Catholicism, where, during the Middle Ages and Renaissance, women were confined to one of two roles: that of a nun or a wife. Women who exhibited abnegation, sacrifice, and total devotion to Jesus Christ were viewed, per this philosophy, as fonts of religious and spiritual strength. Among Latinos, mothers are represented as a center of spiritual gravity.

### What kind of support do mothers get from the community?

We should start by addressing the reverse of this question. The maternal figure in Hispanic culture is understood as a bastion of endurance and continuity. On May 10, the Spanish-speaking world celebrates Mother's Day. The holiday takes place on varying dates in the United States.

### What about single-parent families?

The stereotype of the single-mother family is pervasive. Since colonial times, the absence of the father figure is a social, psychological, and cultural feature among Latinos.

Yet nontraditional families are the result of a myriad of forces. A number of factors determine the solvency of the family as a strong unit among Latinos, among them economics, immigration, health, gender, and education. In the 1980s, the increase in divorces among Latinos and the rampant drug addiction among the poor multiplied the number of single-parent units. On the other hand, stereotypes always have a hold in reality. Single-parent families have a long history in Latin America, as fathers, for a variety of social, psychological, and sexual reasons, have absented themselves from the household.

### Are divorces frequent?

Divorce has been legalized only recently in a number of Latin American countries. The rate of divorces among Latinos in the United States has multiplied visibly since the 1980s.

## How does the Latino community view abortion?

Latino attitudes on abortion vary depending on the age of individuals. The older people are, the more conservative their beliefs tend to be on the topic. Younger people tend to be more liberal, even though, as a result of the pervasiveness of Catholicism, abortion is not widely endorsed in the community.

## How do Latinos see childhood?

Hispanic culture reveres the relationship between child and mother. Childhood is understood in the culture as an impressionable developmental stage in which the individual absorbs the moral values needed to function in society. This occurs through a series of institutions: the family first and foremost, the school, and the religious center.

Due to increased immigration to the United States, the population of children in the Hispanic community has increased faster than in any other ethnic group, growing from 9% of the nation's total population in 1980 to 16% in 1999. In the first decade of the 21st century, 35% of the Latino population consists of children. This number is expected to at least remain steady by 2025.

## What are the challenges Latino children face?

Poverty runs rampant among Latinos, and children pay a heavy price for it. In 2000, a stunning 27% of Latino children under the age of 18 lived in poverty. By 2014, the number had gone down just a bit: 23.6% of Latino children were poor, compared with 10.1% of the non-Latino white population. Poverty was more prevalent in single-parent homes.

Language and cultural limitations put Latino children at a disadvantage in school, and drop-out rates increase during adolescence. In order to make ends meet, parents are often employed in two, even three, jobs per person, and children may be left unattended. This has a variety of ramifications.

### Is there child labor among Latinos?

Although prohibited by law in the United States, child labor is a common practice among Latinos, particularly in agriculture. The total number is difficult to grasp. According to the United Farm Workers, around 800,000 children were employed in the United States in 2000. The US Government Accountability Office put it at 300,000 and the Census Bureau at 155,000. Children might begin working at the age of 12. Aside from the danger and exhaustion that children experience working in agriculture, they are also exposed to pesticides. Sanitation conditions are distressing as is the interrupted, and otherwise, limited access to education and to family quality time.

### What are the illnesses affecting children?

The one requiring urgent attention is diabetes. The diet of working-class Latino children is irregular. Thus, there is an astonishingly high incidence of type 2 diabetes among them and, for that matter, among the minority in general. In 2014, a study showed that the prevalence of "total" diabetes, that is, diagnosed and undiagnosed, among Latinos was approximately 16.9% for both men and women, significantly higher than the 10.2% for non-white Latinos. The study also pointed out that such incidence varies from one subgroup to another: Mexican Americans had a prevalence of 18.3%; Dominican Americans and Puerto Ricans, 8.1%; Central Americans, 17.7%; Cuban Americans, 13.4%; and South Americans, 10.2%.

### What about adolescent gangs?

Adolescence is a period of transition. As the body undergoes changes, the individual also seeks to understand what role to play in society. With the breakup of the ethnic family among the poor, the adolescent looks for ways to validate individual identity by forming partnerships with other disenfranchised youths. In urban environments, the result is the creation of support groups whose objective might be loose enough as to become violent. This is the phenomenon of the *gangas*, the Spanglish word for gangs.

Gangs have a political, aesthetic, moral, gender, and psychological component. Reacting to the oppressiveness of the environment, these youths are eager to receive attention. When they are ignored, they turn their animosity into a statement of being. It is important to remember that gangs date back to the early parts of the 19th century. Some historians have referred to seditious, even revolutionary, adolescent entities who resisted the Treaty of Guadalupe Hidalgo, the Spanish-American Wars, and other turning points by reacting in nonofficial ways.

Among the dozens of Latino gangs are MS-13, Playboys, White Fence, Fresno Bulldogs, Dominicans Don't Play, Northside Bolen Parque 13, Ñetas, Pomona 12th Street Sharkies, Varrio Nuevo Estrada, Logan Heights Gang, and Sureños.

### Is ideology always defined?

*Gangas* often dismiss political channels as a way to express their motives. Their interest is in loyalty, tradition, and turf. Latino gangs fight for control of a particular urban territory. They honor their leaders in a tribal fashion, through a system of gifts and recompense. They distinguish themselves from other gangs through their choice of dress and through public symbols and a type of self-created graffiti language, which they stamp on public spaces. They evade police attention by gathering at night, during weekends, and at unusual hours.

### Do gangs have fixed internal structures?

Their organization is quite specific. The choice of leadership is never random. It has to do with courage and loyalty. There are cultural differences between West Coast and East Coast gangs, and between Chicano and Puerto Rican gangs. Those differences might have to do with their initiation rites. For a member to be initiated into a gang, a series of well-specified yet improvised events need to take place. Some of these events might have a sexual component. Male and female gangs take different approaches to initiation.

The participation of an adolescent in a gang may generate family conflict. That conflict is often shaped across generational lines. Plus, gangs are often involved with drugs as well as criminal activity.

### Is gang participation among Latino youths higher than among other minorities?

Such has been the publicity of Latino gangs since World War II that these groups already have a place in history. There are movies about them (*American Me* [1992] with Edward James Olmos and *Blood In, Blood Out* [1993], directed by Taylor Hackford) and books (Luis J. Rodriguez's *Always Running: La Vida Loca, Gang Days in L.A.* [1993] and its sequel, *It Calls You Back: An Odyssey through Love, Addiction, Revolutions, and Healing* [2011]). Less ethnicized representations are available in musicals like Stephen Sondheim and Leonard Bernstein's *West Side Story*. The incidence of gang participation appears to be higher among ethnic minorities in the past few decades, whereas in the early part of the 20th century, Irish, Jews, and Italians also used to be involved in gang activities. According to the National Gang Center, a project funded by the US Department of Justice's Office of Juvenile Justice and Delinquency Prevention and the Bureau of Justice Assistance, 46% of gang members in the United States are of Latino background, in contrast with 35% of blacks, 11% of whites, and 7% of other ethnicities. But economics, as well as ethnicity, plays the larger role. Insofar as a portion of the population is disenfranchised with the mainstream, ways to express frustration are sought. But economics and ethnicity alone are not enough. Hormones are also important. Adolescence is a difficult and unsettling stage of life in general.

### What about incarceration?

The demographic ciphers of incarcerated Latinos—especially young men—is high: in 2010, 19% of those in prison had a Hispanic background, meaning almost one out of every five. The staggering number (at the time, Latinos constituted 16% of the overall national population) suggested that a large amount of Latino adults, and within it considerably more men than women, had the experience of prison as a formative element in their adult life.

Among Latinos, Puerto Ricans have the highest incarceration rate, followed by Mexicans.

During the 2016 presidential campaign, Donald Trump used this statistic to frequently portray undocumented immigrants as criminals, which was a misrepresentation. He argued that deporting them was a way to empty the nation of Latino delinquents who had come to create havoc. The fact is that undocumented immigrants to the United States do not usually go through the prison system. Instead, they had been deported immediately by the George W. Bush and Barack Obama administrations.

### Is sexuality a forbidden topic among Latinos?

The family in Latino culture tends to be a tight, conservative nuclear unit. Religion keeps the topics of sexuality and eroticism off the kitchen table. Only when discussing them as a biological means of reproduction are they not portrayed as dirty and forbidden. However, as the minority becomes more acclimated to the American way of life, a more liberal approach seems to be coming to the fore.

*What is the approach to abortion and birth control?*

The approach is multifaceted. Religious upbringing manifests itself in a conservative view of abortion, even though it is estimated that between 1990 and 2000 Latinos accounted for two million abortions. At the end of that period, Latina women represented 12.8% of the US population yet accounted for 20.1% of abortions in the nation. There are differences within the Latino minority when it comes to the topic. Cuban Americans tend to be more pro-choice.

Birth control is also a debated issue. Catholicism advocates only natural birth-control methods. Yet other methods are far more popular and are increasingly accepted: the pill, the condom, the diaphragm, and sterilization. The spread of AIDS and some venereal diseases among Latinos has changed people's views, particularly with regard to safety and hygiene.

*How do Latinos understand homosexuality?*

Homosexuality is the reverse of machismo. It remains taboo. Gays, both female and male, are often ridiculed, ostracized, even attacked by family, acquaintances, and strangers. Derogatory words to refer to them include, for gays, *joto, puto*, and *maricón*; for lesbians, *hombrecita* and *marimacha*. But attitudes are changing. Latinos within the second and third generations are less xenophobic. Among others, the Mexican and Chicano folktale of *La Llorona*, the Hollering Woman, has been used by feminists to denounce homophobia.

There are a number of artistic and literary representations about gay people that have helped educate the public. Through his work, the photographer Andrés Serrano, who is of Honduran descent and a recipient of a National Endowment for the Arts fellowship, has pushed the topic to the fore. He is known for his images of corpses and particularly for the polemical *Piss Christ*, a photo of a crucifix submerged in the artist's urine. In 1989, Senator Alfonse D'Amato of New York spoke in Congress against using taxpayer money to support sacrilegious art of Serrano's kind. Under pressure, the National Gallery, where the image was being shown, closed the exhibit. The topic is also discussed in books like the prominent Chicana thinker Gloria Anzaldúa's *Borderlands/La Frontera* (1987), as well as John Rechy's *City of Night* (1963), Achy Obejas's *We Came All the Way from Cuba So You Could Dress Like This?* (1994), Jaime Manrique's *Eminent Maricones* (1999), and Francisco X. Alarcón's *From the Other Side of Night/Del otro lado de la noche* (2008), as well as in the work of the essayist Richard Rodriguez.

### Who was Gloria Anzaldúa?

She was an incisive, thought-provoking feminist intellectual whose work meditates on *mestizaje* in ways that carry the topic beyond Vasconcelos's views on miscegenation. In Anzaldúa's viewpoint, mestizos, especially mestizas, carry with themselves the burden of a history marked by the injury of colonialism. She explored the intersection of language, culture, and history from a radical viewpoint.

Aside from *Borderlands/La Frontera*, her views are presented in *This Bridge Called My Back: Writings by Radical Women of Color* (1981), *Making Face/Making Soul/Haciendo Caras: Creative and Critical Perspectives by Feminists of Color* (1990), *Interviews/ Entrevistas* (2000), and *Light in the Dark/Luz en lo oscuro: Rewriting Identity, Spirituality, Reality* (2015).

### Who is Richard Rodriguez?

Rodriguez is one of the most controversial intellectuals in the Latino minority. Born in 1944, his debut autobiography, *Hunger of Memory*, was an attack on bilingual education. It was published in 1982 and was quickly attacked by a generation trying to find a balance between languages (English and Spanish) and between cultures (Anglo and Hispanic). Rodriguez also came out against affirmative action. One of the sections of his volume is about being offered a scholarship as a Mexican American and declining it because he believed he wasn't receiving it out of talent but as a result of his ethnicity.

He has also written several other books, including *Days of Obligation: An Argument with My Mexican Father* (1992), *Brown: The Last Discovery of America* (2002), and *Darling: A Spiritual Autobiography* (2013). The four form a kind of tetralogy about the changing faces of America at the turn of the 21st century. Rodriguez also worked as a commentator for PBS.

He came out as gay in *Days of Obligation*. While some readers applauded him, others reacted negatively to the fact that in his previous book he had not acknowledged his sexuality. He isn't actively involved in the gay rights movement, which has been another source of criticism.

### What are the challenges of the Latino LGBTQ community?

They are significant ones. While change is evident not only in the United States but also in Latin America, the Latino minority remains staunchly conservative when it comes to nontraditional gender roles. The LGBTQ community is often bullied, targeted, and otherwise marginalized.

### Is marriage a strong institution?

In comparison with other ethnic groups, Latinos appear to remain overwhelmingly supportive of marriage as a civil and religious union. Couples living together prior to marriage is not a common practice, although it is likely to become one as Latinos assimilate into the American mainstream.

### What about the elderly?

Because the nuclear family among Latinos remains strong, a separation of parents and children, compared to the traditional

American model, is less strenuous. The elderly tend to live with the family until death. They are called to participate in child care, cooking, religious worship, and educational activities.

### What is the Latino concept of death?

Needless to say, death plays an integral role in the life of any civilization. Burial sites, funerals, mourning rituals, and the connection between the living and the deceased differ dramatically from one culture to another. In their heterogeneity, Latinos have different approaches.

### Have these concepts changed throughout time?

Pre-Columbian tribes like the Nahuatl believed in the afterlife. They believed death was part of a natural cycle. Among the Aztecs the way a person lived and died was crucial. Soldiers who perished on the battlefield, it was thought, entered a special sphere, as did women who died during pregnancy. Across history, the behaviors, customs, and rites surrounding death in Hispanic civilization are not the same.

Pre-Columbian views changed in their intercourse with Iberian culture. The Spaniards were engaged in rituals based on the Passion story. To suffer in life is to achieve a better life after death. Furthermore, there is the conviction in Hispanic Catholicism that after death there are a heaven and a hell. According to what an individual might have done in moral terms in life, the former is seen as a reward and the latter as punishment.

The combination of the two has produced holidays like Día de los Muertos, the Day of the Dead, also known as All Saint's Day, celebrated on November 1 and 2, in which Mexican Americans spend the night in cemeteries eating, chatting, and commemorating their deceased friends and family. As Latinos assimilate in the United States, these rituals are once again being transformed.

## What kinds of representations of death are available in Latino culture?

The *calavera* is an all-pervading pop symbol in Latino culture. It appears on stickers, posters, key chains, cartoons, piñatas, and T-shirts. It is also present in murals and paintings. José Guadalupe Posada, a 19th-century Mexican engraver, popularized the symbol by using it on cartoons, posters, and greeting cards. Frida Kahlo constantly makes use of it in her art. Death even appears in *pastorelas*, or Nativity plays staged during the Christmas season. In movies, it is present in Luis Valdez's *Zoot Suit* (1978), and in literature it is explored in books like *The Labyrinth of Solitude* (1950) and *The Hispanic Condition* (1995).

Linked to the *calavera* as folklore manifestation is the legend of the stolen skull of the Mexican revolutionary hero Pancho Villa. Apparently Villa's tomb in Parral, Chihuahua, was raided on February 6, 1926, three years after Villa was assassinated, and his skull was stolen. Other parts of the body might have been taken as well. The whereabouts of the skull in particular has become the stuff of legend. At one point it was said to be in the headquarters of the Skull and Bones, an undergraduate senior secret club at Yale University that started in 1832—and that President George W. Bush's grandfather, Prescott Bush, brought it there. Villa's skull is occasionally reproduced in *calaveras*, one in an array of playful possibilities through which the Mexican population plays with parody. Other *calaveras* supposedly belong to Hernán Cortés, La Malinche, Diego Rivera, and Frida Kahlo.

## Are Latinos people of deep-seated faith?

Faith plays a major role in the lives of 450 million Spanish-language people in the entire world. Catholicism was brought by the Spaniards and Portuguese to the New World but it didn't spread in pure form. Its encounter with aboriginal practices in the Americas resulted in religious transculturation, a phenomenon whereby elements of the conqueror's religious rituals and those of the vanquished intertwine. Enter a church in San José, Medellín, or Caracas and you'll notice the graphic suffering of Jesus Christ. You'll also come across an abundance of saints, which to some historians of religion is a remnant of idolatry. Other faiths are present among Latinos in the United States, among them Judaism, Islam, and Buddhism. In all cases, religion helps define, even tangentially, almost every aspect of life, from education to sexuality.

### What was the status of Catholicism in Spain in 1492?

At that time, Spain was bringing to a close its effort at *la reconquista*. After a period of cohabitation, the Jews and the Muslims were expelled from the Iberian Peninsula: the Jews in 1492, shortly after the Muslims were expelled from Granada. Those refusing to become full-fledged Catholics through conversion, as well as those accused of being witches, evil worshipers, or homosexuals or of performing other "deviant behavior," were persecuted by the Holy Office of the Inquisition. The conquistadors and missionaries in the New World were devout Catholics: the former used military force, the latter used physical force. Their quest was to spread the gospel, which they saw as the essential tool to "civilize" the Indians. In their eyes, the natives were idolatrous pagans. They committed themselves to *catecism*, or the teaching of the New Testament, and believed that the Bible justified their actions.

### What kinds of religion existed in the Americas in pre-Columbian civilization?

In the mid-15th century, the two largest empires in the Americas were the Aztecs in Mesoamerica and the Incas in the Andean region. Their religion was polytheistic, that is, built around a plethora of deities.

*What happened to the aboriginal religions in the colonial period?*

They were synthesized into a fresh mix. Ethnographers describe the process as transculturation. Elements of pre-Columbian practices endure in the idiosyncratic form of Catholicism in the Spanish-speaking world.

*When did Catholicism become the preeminent*
*faith among Latinos in the United States?*

The first explorers to Florida, Louisiana, Texas, and California were Catholics. By the 16th century, missions were established from Florida to California in places like San Agustin, San Diego, San Luis Obispo, and San Jose. The result is that by the mid-19th century, when the Treaty of Guadalupe Hidalgo and the Gadsden Purchase were signed, the population of the Southwest was predominantly Catholic. That, along with the immigration of large masses of Catholics, has defined the religious persuasion of Latinos.

*What are the characteristics of Hispanic*
*Catholicism in the Americas?*

There is, for one thing, an abundance of saints. The iconography of Jesus Christ is also more graphic than in other traditions of Catholicism. Depictions of his suffering on the Cross tend to emphasize his wounds and to include more blood. A quick visit to a cathedral in San Juan, Caracas, or Bogotá provides proof of this.

*What Spanish versions of the Bible circulated in the New World?*

In 1551 an edict by the Holy Office of the Inquisition forbade the translation of the Old and New Testaments into Spanish. But it didn't stop anyone from embarking on the projects. The earliest Spanish version used in the Americas, written by Juan

Pérez de Pineda, is known as *Biblia del Oso* and was originally published in 1569 in Basel, Switzerland.

Through the missions like the one in Saint Agustin, Iberian priests taught the Indians ethics and simultaneously brought them to the Christian faith. They predominantly used Pérez de Pineda's version in their enterprise up until the age of independence in 1810, when Father Miguel Hidalgo y Costilla, a Catholic priest, incited the population of New Spain (as Mexico was known in the 18th century) to secede from the Iberian Peninsula. Since then, a variety of other translations, for the most part produced in Spain (although a couple of examples come from Mexico and Argentina), have come from outside.

### Which is the most popular?

The so-called Reina Valera, made in 1909, is seen by millions of Catholics as *"la palabra de Dios en español,"* or the word of God in Spanish.

### What is Guadalupanismo?

Mexican Catholicism rotates around the image of the Virgin of Guadalupe, which was already widespread during colonial times but acquired nationalistic overtones during the war of independence in 1810. At this time, Father Miguel Hidalgo y Costilla, the leader of the rebellion against Spain, literally rang the bell of freedom—*el grito de Dolores*—and marched with a banner of the Virgin of Guadalupe. Subsequently, her image was used by Pancho Villa, Emiliano Zapata, and other revolutionary figures. Politicos too embrace her. The iconography around her touches every aspect of society, even beyond economic, political, and ethnic lines. Her image appears in movies and songs and on calendars, cigarette boxes, T-shirts, coffee mugs, and so on.

### How did the Virgin of Guadalupe acquire her national stature?

According to a legend, on December 12, 1531, about a decade after the fall of Tenochtitlán, the Aztec capital, at the hands of the Spanish conqueror Hernán Cortés, the Virgin, eventually called the "Queen of Mexico" and "Empress of the Americans" (other names include La Virgen de Tepeyac, Santa María de Guadalupe, La Criolla, La Guadalupana, La Virgen Ranchera, La Morena, La Criolla, and La Pastora), appeared to an indigenous peasant called Juan Diego in Mount Tepeyac, near what is Mexico City today. The legend says that he saw her in what was a shrine for the Aztec goddess Tonantzin. He heard some singing voices and then she appeared, telling him she was the Virgin Mary. Her silhouette, with a halo, appeared a total of seven times. The Virgin told Juan Diego to visit the bishop of Mexico City, Juan de Zumárraga, and request that he build a temple in her honor. The temple, she said, would celebrate her embrace of the Mexican people. She promised to support them in their misery. Juan Diego visited Zumárraga but was chided by him and his entourage. Then he returned to the site where the Virgin appeared and told her of the rejection he had received. The Virgin asked him to pick some roses from a bush nearby that seldom bloomed at that time of year, put them in a cloak, and take them to the bishop. When Juan Diego removed the roses from the cloak in front of Zumárraga, the image of the Virgin appeared on the cloak. That became proof of Juan Diego's claim. A temple was subsequently built, and the Virgin of Guadalupe was canonized as the principal Catholic symbol of Mexico.

### What is her appeal?

Theologically, it is important to remember that Mary's role in the New Testament, which includes four gospels, is relatively limited. In other gospels left out of the canonical text of the Christian Church she might have been more relevant. The Trinity—the Father, the Son, and the Holy Ghost—command the full attention, with Jesus Christ in the lead part. In other words, the New Testament downplays the female aspect of the Passion. In Mexico Mary is an elevated figure and is, in her aboriginal incarnation, proof of the archetypal relevance of the mother.

Most significant is the fact that the Virgin of Guadalupe is a *mestiza*. In Mexican religious iconography, her body, with the exception of her face and hands, is shown covered. But her face and hands are invariably brown-skinned. Thus, the Mexican variant of Catholicism was adapted, in terms of ethnicity and gender, to the needs of a mixed-race population. It also depicts her, from the outset of her dialogue with Juan Diego, as embracing the humble and impoverished.

### What is the connection between the Virgin of Guadalupe and Latinos?

Her status as the "Queen of Mexico" has expanded to "Mother of Chicanos." All across the Southwest, her image is displayed by Mexican Americans on major holidays and is widespread on Mexico's Day of Independence, which takes place on September 16. It also appears on Cesar Chavez Day, celebrated on March 31. In literature, she is present in *Bless Me, Ultima* (1972), the novel by Rudolfo Anaya, the story of a young man and his relationship with a *curandera* who becomes his mentor.

### Did the United Farm Workers adopt her image?

The civil rights leader Cesar Chavez, a devout Catholic, displayed her image during labor strikes, right next to the union flag. Thus, the Virgin of Guadalupe became intimately associated with the struggle for justice and equality during the Chicano movement.

### Are there other Virgins?

The Virgen de la Caridad del Cobre (the Virgin of Charity) is the matron saint of Cuba and at the core of Afro-Caribbean religion. She too is a by-product of transculturation. She originated in the 17th century and became a national icon in 1916, after the Spanish-American War. Emerging from the crossroads of Catholicism and Yoruba traditions, Pope John Paul II officially crowned her on January 24, 1998, in Santiago de Cuba.

She is almost always portrayed with three children at her feet. Myth has it that three 10-year-old boys, two indigenous and one a black slave, found a statue of the Virgen de la Caridad del Cobre around 1607, on their way from the village of Barajagua to Nipe Bay in search of salt to cure meat. They are called the three Juanes. Once they returned to their village, they placed the statue in a hermitage. The statue would disappear overnight and reappear in the morning. This happened seven times. The villagers interpreted the event as a sign that she wanted to be placed in a better site. She was moved near the copper mines, where a basilica was built.

### What ethnic identity does she have?

At times she is represented as a *mestiza* and at others as a mulatto.

### What is her link to African traditions?

The region where she was placed was inhabited by African slaves who imbued their prayers with animistic elements. The Virgen de la Caridad del Cobre is an incarnation of Ochún, a central figure in Santería practices.

### What is Santería?

Also known as Regla de Ocha, it is a widespread variety of Afro-Caribbean religion practiced in Cuba, with Yoruba origins mixed with Catholic elements. During the colonial period, there were Church-sponsored institutions known as *cabildos* designed as support groups. The autonomy that African slaves were given in these *cabildos* encouraged them to develop their own practices. They paired images of Jesus Christ and the Virgin Mary with deities known as *orishas*. For almost every Catholic saint there is an *orisha*. The roster of *orishas* includes Ochún, the goddess of water and sensuality; Obatalá, the god of purity and justice; and Babalú Ayé, a god of morality and healing. The central divine figure is Olodumare. Their veneration by worshipers, called *santeros*, allows for interference in natural and human affairs. Rituals include dances with frantic physical movements and animal sacrifice.

### Are ghosts a fixture in Latino life?

Beyond the religious differences at the heart of the minority, death is perceived as a continuation, not an interruption, of life. Take the Day of the Dead. Known in Spanish as Día de los Muertos, it is celebrated on November 1st and 2nd, that is, around Halloween time. The holiday is predominantly a Mexican and Central American celebration, popular in the Southwest and along the US-Mexico border. Families traditionally spend a night at the cemetery near the tomb of their beloved deceased, picnicking and sleeping at the place. Colorful *calaveras*, or sugar skulls, animate the festivities. Artistic references to the Day of the Dead range from Malcolm Lowry's novel *Under the Volcano* (1947) to Frida Kahlo's self-portraits.

The idea of the graveyard as a terrifying place is not ingrained in the culture. In other words, the dead, in the form of ghosts, are not perceived to hunt the living. Instead, they are seen as counselors with whom one sustains an ongoing dialogue. In people's opinion, spirits manifest themselves through dreams, visions, and even in daily life.

### What about Protestantism?

Its influence in Latin America has been on the rise since the dictatorship of Porfirio Díaz in Mexico. It was also brought to the Caribbean Basin and Central America by American soldiers during the Spanish-American War and in the different invasions of the 20th century. Evangelicals have made inroads, especially the faction known as Pentecostals, through missionary work.

The use of TV as a tool for spreading Protestantism has become quite successful. It is estimated that at the end of the 20th century 15.5% of Mexican Americans were Protestants, as well as 10.2% of Cuban Americans, and 10% of Puerto Ricans on the mainland. The expansion is a direct response to the erosion of Catholicism, which has suffered from sex and corruption scandals. It might also be a consequence of the multiplication of religious choices for the general population.

### Are there Jews in Latin America?

There are approximately 400,000 Jews in the Spanish- and Portuguese-speaking countries on this side of the Atlantic Ocean. The largest concentration is in Argentina, where a sizable immigrant wave from Eastern Europe (Poland, Lithuania, Ukraine, Belarus, and so on) and Russia settled between 1880 and 1920. Jews then settled in Brazil and Mexico. In colonial times, Mexico and Peru were the most cosmopolitan centers in the hemisphere and crypto-Jews—individuals who kept their Judaism secret out of fear of the Inquisition—were known to live in both countries.

I am a Mexican Jew. My ancestors came from Poland, Ukraine, and Belarus and settled in Mexico at the dawn of the 20th century. I grew up speaking Yiddish and Spanish. I have written about my education, and about switching languages in life, in my memoir, *On Borrowed Words* (2001). The movie *My Mexican Shivah* (2007), based on a short story I wrote, also deals with this topic.

*What percentage of Latinos in the United States is Jewish?*

The Census Bureau doesn't catalogue people according to religion. Still, the answer, according to other sources, is less than 1%. According to the Anti-Defamation League, a Jewish organization, close to 50% of Latino immigrants to the United States hold strong anti-Semitic opinions. That percentage decreases in the second generation, and even more in the following one.

*How about the number of Arabs?*

The role that Arabs played for centuries in the history of the Iberian Peninsula is enormous. Spanish cuisine, art, dance, and architecture manifest that influence. The Spanish language does too: words like *almohada* and *zanahoria* have Arab roots. After the Crusades and *la reconquista*, the Muslim religion became marginalized, its history unacknowledged. But the Americas, through conquest, were inheritors of that secret heritage. In modern times, Arab immigrants from Egypt, Syria, Lebanon, Iraq, and elsewhere have established themselves in countries as different as Argentina, Colombia, and Mexico. Their communities were small in size. Islam is also making inroads, albeit in limited fashion, among Latinos. In 2017, with statistics still unreliable, there are believed to be between 40,000 and 200,000 Muslim Latinos in the United States, a number that acquires added significance when one considers that Latin America, which has one of the largest Arab diasporas in the world, has between 17 to 30 million Arab people (Brazil alone has approximately 10 million), not all of whom are, of course, Muslim. The richest man in the world is part of this diaspora: Carlos Slim of Mexico. Organizations like the Latino American Dawah, created in 1997 in New York City, are devoted to education about the Muslim world, in particular about its main religion.

### When was the Qur'an translated into Spanish and available in the United States?

The central Islamic text was translated into Latin by Peter the Venerable, Abbot of Cluny and the first Christian to study Islamic sources in earnest fashion, in the 12th century. It was rendered for the first time in Spanish—and only partially—in the 19th century.

In the United States there are several available translations. There is one made in Argentina by Ahmed Abboud and Rafael Castellanos and known as *El Sagrado Corán* (1953). Another one is by Abdel Ghani Melara Navio: *Traducción y comentario del Noble Corán* (1979). The most popular version is Julio Cortés Soroa's *El Corán* (1980), published under the aegis of the Tahrike Tarsile Qur'an in New York. Cortés Soroa, a Spaniard, taught at the University of North Carolina at Chapel Hill. Finally, there is the translation by Kamel Mustafa Hallak, called *El Corán Sagrado* (1997), printed by Amana Publications.

### How many Latino Jews are there?

Again, the numbers are unreliable. A 2016 survey suggested that there are some 200,000 Latino Jews in the United States, that is, Latinos who were born Jewish, converted, or immigrated from Latin America and elsewhere. This is unlikely given that Latin America as a whole only has about half a million Jews altogether, with Argentina as the site of the largest concentration, followed by Brazil and Mexico. The same survey portrayed this population as highly educated, with seven out of ten Latino Jewish households earning more than $100,000 annually, when compared to 30% of American Jewish households.

There is, indeed, a growing literature on this topic by authors like Marjorie Agosín, Ruth Behar, Victor Perera, and Ariel Dorfman, which includes memoirs like *A Cross and a Star* (1994), *The Cross and the Pear Tree* (1995), *Heading South,*

*Looking North, On Borrowed Words* (2001), and *An Island Called Home* (2007).

### What role do indigenous practices play among Latinos?

In spite of a history of oppression, indigenous practices survive, often with a strong Catholic emphasis. They are frequently shamanic. Anthropologists have studied their retention and have found that as Western ways of life have become more homogeneous, these practices have provided an alluring alternative. People seek them for medical, religious, and dietary purposes, among others.

### What about Afro-Caribbean beliefs?

The same goes for Afro-Caribbean beliefs. For instance, Santería is a religious factor in Cuba and other places in the Caribbean Basin and is practiced by immigrants from these regions in the United States.

### Are younger Latinos less religious?

In general, in the United States second-generation Latinos are less religious, especially those whose parents were immigrants. But the trend doesn't hold because Latino adults tend to reconnect with faith later on in life. However, trends show that the type of religiosity does change from one generation to the next, becoming more flexible.

# 6

# FUSIÓN LATINA

### What is fusión latina?

Spanish-language TV and radio have been instrumental in the forging of a Latino identity—what is called "*fusión latina.*" No other immigrant wave has built a media infrastructure with equal power. And media, of course, shapes behavior. The emblematic marriage of Lucy and Ricky is a paradigm of integration. Latino arts have undergone a bonanza since the 1980s. But the Latino sensibility isn't only available before a microphone and a camera; folklore might well be its most vivid expression. That folklore is evident in a plethora of places, from stand-up comedy like that produced by George Lopez and Carlos Mencia, to cartoons like La Cucaracha, and to marketplaces and festivities like *quinceañeras* and Cinco de Mayo, which commemorates the fierce defense of 4,000 Mexico soldiers against an invading French army on May 5, 1862. It is also present in children's songs and stories.

It is important to look at those cultural manifestations—music, dance, pictorial art, TV, cinema, radio, theater, and literature—on their own terms as well as in toto. I include sports in this manifestation as well, although they are often considered an aspect of culture, not of entertainment.

*Is music the most vibrant of artistic
manifestations among Latinos?*

Yes. It is also the most heterogeneous. From plenas to salsa to
*reggaetón* and jazz, the possibilities of rhythm appear to be infi-
nite. Differences of race and class are often obliterated in music,
as with the motherly icon Celia Cruz, who managed to unite
Caribbeans of all backgrounds by simply saying *"¡Azúcar!"*
Tito Puente made people turn on their feet with his drums. Yet
the music of Latinos is also a record of their plight. And Shakira
combines her Lebanese, Colombian, and American identities to
sing about passion. The Mexican narcocorrido chronicles the
adventures of drug traffickers while the Dominican merengue
tells of immigrants looking for a ticket to the American Dream.
The enthusiasm of fans is evident in concerts and dance clubs.

### What kind of history does Latin music have in the United States?

Music is an invaluable tool for understanding a people.
Since pre-Columbian times, music has played a major role in
Hispanic civilization. Given the heterogeneity of Latinos, it is
no surprise that each national group relates to some genres
and not to others.

### Do different national groups have different musical forms?

Bolero, with roots in an ancient Iberian dance of ternary (three-
beat) rhythms even though today it has a binary (two-beat)
form, is one of the most popular genres. It established its reputation in Cuba in the last third of the 19th century. It wasn't
until the 1940s that it made a crossover for Anglo audiences,
acquiring English-language lyrics and becoming a success in
the United States, first among Caribbean immigrants and their
descendants, and then in the country at large. Conversely, the
*bomba* and plena are the most endeared Puerto Rican musical

forms, reflecting the connection between European and African influences in the Caribbean Basin. And in Mexico, *ranchera* music, often played by mariachi, is said to be an expression of the nation's psyche. It started as a variety of rural music but in the second half of the 20th century made a transition to urban settings. There are classic *ranchera* songs and more experimental variations.

The most important genres in Latin music are corridos, tejano, salsa, bachata, merengue, *reggaetón*, jazz, and hip-hop. The journey made by some musical genres from Latin America to the United States resulted in important modifications. Sometimes these are only recognizable at the thematic level. Lyrics address the plight of immigrants, their quest to find a place away from home, and their loneliness and need for affection. Modifications are also palpable in the use of new instruments, the influence of other musical genres, and the need to adapt to a more diverse audience.

### And classical music?

There are a number of Latino classical musicians whose oeuvre has brought them international reputation. Plácido Domingo, the opera tenor from Mexico, has interpreted every conceivable character from Verdi to Puccini. He has also directed opera.

The list of classical composers includes the Pulitzer Prize winner Mario Davidovsky, Orlando Jacinto García, Ricardo Lorenz, and Osvaldo Golijov. And there is Lalo Schifrin, who has written scores for many movies from *Dirty Harry* (1971) to the *Mission Impossible* series (1996–2018).

### What different instruments are used?

Wind and string instruments are popular, including flute, clarinet, and saxophone, as well as guitar, cello, and bass. Jazz also uses piano. Accordion, drums, harp, and maracas are frequently played too. Each national tradition uses different instruments, which at times travel to the United States. In Cuba, musicians use batas, batijas, bongos, cajón, chekere, claves, congas, guataca, guiro, marimba, palitos, and timbales. Mexico favors marimba, pandero, bajo sexton, and gitarrón. Puerto Rico employs bomba, cuatro, guicharo, and panderetas. Argentina uses the bandoneón. And the Dominican Republic is known for the gira and tambora.

### What is a corrido?

Etymologically, the word corrido comes from the Spanish infinitive *correr*, to run. It is used to describe a border ballad about a legendary hero or historical event. The origin of the corrido might date back to the medieval Spanish *romancero*. In Mexico there have been *corridistas*, makers of these types of songs, since the war of independence in the early 19th century. There are also those who trust that in the Americas the tradition reaches into the pre-Columbian past. On the US-Mexico border, there are songs about outlaws like Gregorio Cortez and Tiburcio Vásquez, mixing historical and fictional elements, from around the Spanish-American War. These songs told the adventures as acts of resistance and vindication. The structure was fixed, with simple four-line stanzas rhymed at the end and a chorus carrying on a political message. The corridos were delivered anonymously, borrowed from one ballad maker to another, usually accompanied by a strong instrument. As the *corridista* recited them from memory, elements were changed according to the singer's needs.

### Does the tradition continue?

Today there are corridos about President John F. Kennedy, Cesar Chavez, and the martyred tejana singer Selena.

### *And* narcocorridos?

With the growth of the illegal drug trade in the 1990s, a different form of corrido took shape in the United States, especially among Mexican American labor workers. Its themes concentrated on illegal immigrants, the drug cartel, and the run-ins with the US border and police patrol. Among the most famous *narcocorridistas* are Chalino Sánchez and the group Los Tigres del Norte.

### *What about* tejano *and* conjunto *music?*

In Spanish the word conjunto might be understood to mean "band." Conjunto music is a variety of tejano music that includes influences of Mexican music from the northern (*norteño*) part of the country and South Texas and also from black and immigrant rhythms from the Czechs, the Poles, the Germans, and the Italians.

### *Who was Selena?*

Selena, née Selena Quintanilla, born in Houston in 1971, was a prodigious *tejana* singer killed by one of her staffers in 1995. She came from a humble background and began singing in her family's restaurant. When she moved to Corpus Christi, Texas, she, with a soulful soprano voice, formed a group called Selena y los Dinos with her sister and brother. She mixed *Tejano* music with *cumbias*. She also did polkas, ballads, and romantic music. Her first record was *Ven Conmigo*, released in 1990. Her second one, *Amor Prohibido*, which came out four years later, was a huge success. And at the time of her death she was about to release *Dreaming of You*, a crossover album designed to expand her English-language base. The record appeared posthumously. A former employee, who had been president of her fan club and had been suspected of stealing money, shot her at a hotel in Corpus Christi. A film bio, with Jennifer Lopez as Selena, was released in 1997.

## What are plenas?

They are musical pieces, made of syncopated rhythms, that are popular among Puerto Ricans. They use call-and-response vocal cadences and address current social issues. They are a relative of the *bomba*. The first plena was recorded in New York City in 1927. As time goes by, other more popular rhythms, like salsa and *meringue*, have eclipsed it.

## Is there a difference between merengue and bachata in the Caribbean and in the United States?

Merengue has been described as "the prime maker of ethnic identity for Dominicans in the diaspora." Musicians in New York use merengue but incorporate elements from other types of music found in the United States. Their lyrics recount stories of assimilation and nostalgia. Another similar music form is the bachata, which Juan Luis Guerra and his group Los 4.40 turned into an international sensation. Their music was about displacement but also about uncontrolled passion.

## What kind of influence has Brazil exerted in Latino music?

Samba, bossa nova, baião, tropicália, and other rhythms have exerted a powerful influence. Brazil itself, like the Caribbean, brings together musical influences from Africa and the aboriginal population in a fusion at once traditional and invigorating. Samba, popularized by Carmen Miranda, highlights the racial and cultural mix. The extraordinary talent of figures like Caetano Veloso, Gilberto Gil, Chico Buarque, Jorge Ben, and Milton Nascimento has defined Latino music in the United States.

## What different types of salsa are there?

Salsa is not a particular type of music. Instead, it is, according to the musicologist Cristóbal Díaz-Ayala, "a way, a mode of making music." It combines elements from blues, pop, plena, *bomba*, and *guagancó*, among other styles. It developed in New York City in the first half of the 20th century, from the Cuban *son*. Famous salseros include Ray Barretto and Celia Cruz, Charlie and Eddie Palmieri, Johnny Pacheco, La Lupe, and Rubén Blades. Each developed a different repertoire. The Spanish Harlem style of Willie Colón and Daniel Santos is different to the Cuban approach of the Buena Vista Social Club.

### Who was Celia Cruz?

Nicknamed the "Queen of Salsa," she was born in Havana on October 21, 1925, and died in New Jersey on July 16, 2003. Celia Cruz was immensely popular, charismatic, and famous for using the word *¡Azúcar!*, which means sugar in Spanish, to enliven her audience. She made her recording debut while still young with La Sonora Matancera, a famous Cuban band, and sang at clubs like the Tropicana. She left the island in 1960, after Fidel Castro's revolution began to take hold, and settled in Miami and New York City. She recorded some 70 albums and established herself with songs like "*Burundanga*" and "*La negra tiene tumbao.*" Her Afro-Caribbean background is proof that in Latino music ethnic borders can be, if not erased, at least sidestepped. Her funeral was attended by millions of people in Miami.

### What is Latino hip-hop?

Often ridiculed as simply hip-hop recorded by Latino musicians, Latino hip-hop pays tribute to the Puerto Rican roots of the rhythm, which took form in the 1970s in New York City, along with rap and graffiti. It is hip-hop with Spanish lyrics. It evolved through club DJs adapting the music of Tito Puente and others.

## Why is reggaetón so popular?

Also spelled *reguetón*, it is a type of music with origins in Puerto Rico that combines Jamaican dancehall music with *bomba*, plena, and hip-hop. It started in the late 1990s and reached its climax in the early decade of the 21st century.

## Who are the leaders of Latin Jazz?

Latin Jazz is a wing of more traditional jazz that incorporates elements of salsa, merengue, and other Latin rhythms. It is a fusion of Dizzy Gillespie, Charlie Parker, and Miles Davis set in an Afro-Cuban context, and it has evolved to include other national traditions. Musicians are not happy with the term because they feel they are not seen as legitimate as standard jazz musicians. Yet the jazz scene itself has been invigorated by this fusion. It evolved from Brazilian bossa nova as it was mixed with salsa in New York City. Bebo and Chucho Valdés, Danilo Pérez, Chico O'Farrill, Paquito D'Rivera, Gonzalo Rubalcaba, and Omar Sosa have pushed the form to astonishing heights.

## How about dance?

Dance is another favorite pastime of Latinos. Almost every musical rhythm comes along with its deliberate steps, often arranged for couples. The varieties of dance range from montuno, *guaracha*, *jarabe*, mambo, cha-cha-chá, *danzón*, cumbia, *guajira*, *charanga*, plena, *bomba*, and merengue. As in the case of music, the different types of dance are directly linked to their countries of origin. The varieties found in the Dominican Republic—*meringue* and *bachata*—are not practiced in Mexico. Likewise, the *jarabe* is from a particular province of Mexico and remains unknown in the Dominican Republic.

As the assimilation process has evolved, these dances have undergone changes to reflect the impact of Anglo civilization.

The merengue danced in New York City is based on the one from the island, but the stories that animate the US versions are about immigrants. As well, the physical movement is less candid and a bit more inhibited.

### How about dance clubs?

They are a feature of any Latino environment. Depending on the national and ethnic background, one might come across clubs specializing in conjunto music, salseros, *música tropical*, merengue, rock, and *technobanda*.

### Is pictorial art equally important?

Painting by Latinos in the United States is a centuries-old tradition. Religious art abounded in the region of the Southwest during the colonial period, as Christian iconography was a tool used to indoctrinate the aboriginal population. It also incorporated Indian elements. In New Mexico, perhaps the state with the deepest pictorial tradition, there were works in the European style, but also *santeros*, or holy images created for altars in mission churches. Some of these items are called *retablos*, decorated panels that use Catholic iconography. Texas has similar artifacts. The *retablos* are quite popular. People use them as expressions of faith, asking for divine intervention to protect a loved one, be cured from an illness, or improve one's luck on all sorts of levels.

The fact that I've mentioned these two states is not arbitrary. Latino art has evolved across national and geographic lines. Martín Ramírez, a naïf artist—others would describe him as a folk artist—is the by-product of the Mexican Revolution and the migration to California that ensued. His work is different from that of the Cuban American artist Frank García, whose paintings are evocative of Italian renaissance art. In turn, García differs from Nuyorrican painters like Jean-Michel Basquiat, a graffiti artist of Haitian and Puerto Rican descent, who defined his aesthetics in the context of the Afro-Latino influences in New York in the 1970s and 1980s. (He died in 1988, at the age of 28.) These differences ought to preclude any generalizations in terms of technique, themes, or political and religious content.

### How about muralism?

Muralism, as an ideological movement, consolidated its presence in the Spanish-speaking world after the Mexican Revolution of 1910. Artists like Diego Rivera, José Clemente Orozco, and David Alfaro Siqueiros used public spaces, painting frescos on street walls, cafeterias, and music civic centers to call attention to the ancestral desire of the mestizo to find his place in the modern world. They were Marxists by persuasion and expressionist by aesthetic conviction. Their influence reverberated into the United States during the civil rights era. A number of Chicano artists adapted their art into the landscape of the Southwest.

Muralism and graffiti are relatives. Graffiti—from the Italian word *graffito*, and commonly defined as "crude scratching upon public spaces"—might not be as versatile as a mural but it surely contains an equally strong political statement. Its technique uses aerosol paint, applied illegally on urban walls, trains, and other surfaces, at unlikely hours. The act of making graffiti needs to involve danger in order to be considered legitimate. Graffiti artists are also called "writers."

### And street art?

An integral part of the Chicano movement was the graphic art produced around strikes, marches, and other major gatherings. This art was also connected with graffiti and muralism. One of the legacies of the period is the astonishing array of murals by Chicano artists such as Judy Baca, Marcos Raya, Xavier González, José Aceves, René Yáñez, and Yolanda

López, painted on public walls and other venues. The work of three Mexican muralists from the early part of the 20th century—Diego Rivera, José Clemente Orozco, and David Alfaro Siqueiros—serves as inspiration for these murals. Their work was intimately linked to Mexican nationalism and resulted from the armed struggles that swept their country in 1910, known as *la revolución*. The muralists depicted important moments and figures in the country's history in order to raise political awareness. As their influence grew, Rivera, Orozco, and Siqueiros were invited to paint murals in the United States, in places like Detroit, Los Angeles, and New York. The Chicano muralists sought to explore history and myth in the same way, using public space to educate the masses about history. They produced posters in Los Angeles about Aztlán and the Treaty of Guadalupe Hidalgo, with profiles of Cesar Chavez and Dolores Huerta. They also included images of the people, average Chicanos fighting for self-determination.

### And comic strips?

Walt Disney and Hanna Barbera made characters like the Three Caballeros and Speedy González, but Latino cartoon makers produce outside the corporate world. The most significant artists are Lalo Alcaraz, the syndicate cartoonist who created La Cucaracha, featured in the *Los Angeles Times* and other publications, and the brothers Jaime and Gilbert Hernandez, known for the successful alternative comic of the 1980s and 1990s, *Love & Rockets*.

### Is there a particular type of Latino graffiti?

Graffiti evolved in the 1970s and 1980s in big metropolitan centers like New York, Chicago, and Los Angeles. It was the by-product of black, Latino, Chinese, and Korean adolescents in search of expression. It not only coincided with but was part of the same aesthetic that produced hip-hop. Writers tagged their work with ALE, COMET, FUZZ 1, LSD OM, and TAKI 183. Several of them were immigrants from Mexico, El Salvador, Honduras, and the Caribbean Basin. Some incorporated Aztec and Taino elements into their art, while others reflected the plight of Latinos in the United States through references to historical and local figures.

### What are Lowriders?

A lowrider is a type of customized, old-fashioned, ornately decorated automobile with 13-inch wire-spoke wheels, hydraulic systems, and painting and carpentry designs. Fixing up lowriders (also spelled low riders) is a particular hobby in California, an expression of a curated aesthetic denoting a syncretized style.

### What about Latino theater?

Spanish-language theater has been present in the United States since the colonial period, when *actos, pastorelas,* and other religious plays were enacted in the Southwest in plazas and missions. In the 19th century, *carpas,* itinerant theater troupes, entertained the lower class with comic acts. There was also vaudeville. Plus, professional companies from Spain and Latin America toured from one Spanish-language community to another.

The growth of Latino theater took place in the 20th century. In the next page I talk about Teatro Campesino, founded by Luis Valdez during the Chicano movement. In the Northeast, the Repertorio Español and the Puerto Rican Traveling Theater, stationed in New York City, are repertory companies devoted to the dissemination of Hispanic plays. They perform in bilingual format.

Chicano, Cuban, and Puerto Rican playwrights have made their stamp in English on the American stage. Their plays include René Marqués's *La Carreta* (1953), María Irene Fornés's *Fefu and Her Friends* (1977), and Miguel Piñero's *Short Eyes*

(1977), Dolores Prida's *Coser y cantar* (1981), Carlos Morton's *The Many Deaths of Danny Rosales* (1983), and Nilo Cruz's *Anna in the Tropics* (2002). There is also the performance art, with slapstick overtones, of Guillermo Gómez-Peña.

### Who was Luis Valdez?

Luis Valdez is also considered to be a leader of the Chicano movement, but his impact might be seen less at the political than at the artistic level.

Valdez was born in Delano, California, in 1940, to immigrant farm-worker parents. He was already writing for the stage in college, where his play *The Shrunken Head of Pancho Villa* was first produced. After college, he began to volunteer for Cesar Chavez's union, the United Farm Workers. Conscious of the role the arts had in creating political awareness, he founded the Teatro Campesino with farm workers. His objective was to make plays about the plight of Mexican Americans and in support of *la huelga*. In fact, his one-act plays, known as *actos* (in the tradition of medieval Iberian theater), were performed to entertain strikers. Thus, his work had intra-ethnic, activist, and nationalist connotations.

### What are Valdez's most famous plays?

He is best known for *Zoot Suit* (1981), a Brechtian musical about the Los Angeles riots. The play had a successful 11-month run at the Mark Tapper in Los Angeles. It was then transferred to Broadway and ultimately became a film with Edward James Olmos, directed by Valdez himself. Valdez also directed *La Bamba* (1987), a bio film about the singer Ritchie Valens. His other plays include *La gran carpa de la familia Rascuachi, Tiburcio Vasquez*, and *I Don't Have to Show You No Stinking Badges!* Along with the lawyer Oscar "Zeta" Acosta and the journalist Rubén Salazar, Valdez's role in the Chicano movement has legendary proportions.

### How about Lin-Manuel Miranda?

A theater phenomenon is Lin-Manuel Miranda, the creator and actor of *In the Heights* (2008), about Latinos and neighborhood gentrification in Washington Heights. Miranda went on to make what is considered to be one of the most successful Broadway musicals ever: *Hamilton* (2015), a take on the Founding Fathers and the making of the United States through hip-hop music and with a multiethnic cast that portrays Hamilton and others as rough, rowdy, up-and-coming immigrants to the British colonies. Miranda is unquestionably the most important Latino artist in theater to acquire a crossover appeal. I admire his work tremendously. A YouTube video of his wedding in 2010 shows him and his relatives performing "To Life!" from *Fiddler on the Roof* (1964). It is followed by a charmingly playful, semi-improvised, flash-mob performance of the song "96 Thousand" from *In the Heights* in Universal Studies, Los Angeles. The two are ample evidence of Miranda's charm and popularity.

### What about TV?

In successive years, other facets of Spanish-language media also became a major force in the nation's cultural landscape. Radio stations multiplied swiftly almost everywhere. Arguably more important was the impact that Univision and Telemundo had on millions of viewers. By the late 1990s, their growth surpassed their English-language counterparts, ABC, NBC, and CBS.

### Since when have Latinos been active in American television?

The history of Latinos and American television ought to be divided into two: the presence of Latino characters in English-language programs, and Spanish-language TV. In the first category are the 1950s hit *I Love Lucy*, with Lucille Ball and her husband, the Cuban American actor and musician Desi Arnaz, aka Ricky Ricardo. The show lives on, thanks to eternal reruns. Other examples are *Resurrection Boulevard*, *Miami Vice*, *The George Lopez Show*, *American Family*, and *Mind of Mencia*. In the second category are the countless *telenovelas*.

### What is a telenovela?

It is a Spanish-language soap opera, usually broadcast at prime time for an adult audience. The favorite topics are passionate love affairs, machismo and *marianismo*, illegitimate children, and revenge. They usually run for about 25 to 40 episodes. Famous series are *Simplemente María* and *Mi querida Isabel*. Mexico has the monopoly on *telenovelas*; it produces more than any other country, and its telenovelas are watched all around the globe, from Russia to Israel, as well as in Latin America. Venezuela and Brazil also produce their own original material. Since the 1990s, Univision and Telemundo have joined the market. The *telenovelas* produced in Miami and Los Angeles are exclusively geared toward a Latino audience in the United States. The cast of actors might include Puerto Ricans, Colombians, Mexicans, Cubans, and Argentines.

### Who is Jorge Ramos?

Among the most prominent TV journalists is the Mexican-born, Univision anchor Jorge Ramos. He fits into a tradition of activist reporters who see the delivery of news not as factual information delivered in objective ways but as storytelling with an ideological message. Ramos's message isn't so much about endorsing an ideological left or right but about advancing the cause of Latinos in the process of assimilation to American society.

He is the author of a number of books, including *The Other Face of America* (2003), *The Latino Wave* (2005), *The Gift of Time* (2008), and *A Country for All* (2010). Ramos also writes a syndicated newspaper column read throughout the

Spanish-speaking world. He is known for his in-depth interviews with world figures, as well as for his confrontations with politicians in Latin America and the United States, including Donald Trump. His work fits comfortably in the age of politically charged journalism by Fox News and MSNBC.

### What about variety shows on TV?

Spanish-language TV in the United States is known for them. These are programs lasting several hours, usually on the weekend, that feature interviews, musical numbers, comedy skits, and in-studio contests. Arguably the most famous is *Sábado Gigante* in Univision, which started in 1962 and ended in 2015. The host was Don Francisco, a Chilean Jew (a Yiddish speaker) whose real name was Mario Luis Kreutzberger.

### Is there a Latino cinema?

While Spanish-language TV and radio have grown dramatically since the 1960s, Hollywood remains all but closed to Latino filmmakers. To be sure, there have been important movies, such as León Ichaso's *El Super* (1979), Robert Young's *The Ballad of Gregorio Cortez* (1982), Luis Valdez's *Zoot Suit* and *La Bamba*, Ramón Menéndez's *Stand and Deliver* (1988), Gregory Nava's *El Norte* (1984), Ichaso's *Crossover Dreams* (1985), Patricia Cardozo's *Real Women Have Curves* (2002), Eric Eason's *Manito* (2002), and Sergio Arau's *A Day without Mexicans* (2004). Their themes explore issues of isolation, acculturation, and affirmation. When considering the size and importance of the Latino minority in the United States, it is embarrassing that more directors aren't invited to explore relevant issues on the silver screen for an English-speaking audience.

The diversity within the minority also begs the question of whether one could talk, at the outset of the 21st century, of a Latino cinema? Would it not be more pertinent to explore its possibilities across national lines, for example, Chicano, Puerto

Rican, and Cuban cinemas? That is the approach some film critics take. There are B-movie examples, like the *Cheech and Chong* series (1978–1984), geared toward an adolescent audience, that indulge in a type of ethnic humor not always embraceable by the whole minority. Likewise, the work of Luis Valdez is surely contained within the Mexican American tradition.

Among the most successful franchises are Robert Rodriguez's *Spy Kids* (2001–2011), which includes Latino actors and characters.

### What about Latino actors in Hollywood?

The stream goes from Rita Hayworth (née Margarita Cansino) to Chita Rivera, Rita Moreno, Carmen Miranda, and Anthony Quinn to Antonio Banderas and Jennifer Lopez, aka JLo. Their ethnicity might have been a springboard for them but little of what they've tackled in their careers pertains to the Latino experience. Yes, Rita Moreno, a Puerto Rican, was in *West Side Story*, a musical film made in 1961, based on a Broadway hit, about the clash of Italian and Puerto Rican gangs in New York at midcentury. Quinn, of Mexican descent, did *Viva Zapata!* (1952) with Marlon Brando and *The Children of Sánchez* (1978). Banderas revived the *Zorro* franchise (1998–2005), about a New Mexico folk hero of the colonial period. And JLo impersonated the *tejana* singer Selena (1997). Still, these efforts are not appropriate to describe these efforts as encompassing a Latino acting method.

### And radio?

As in the case of TV, Latino radio, the "invisible" medium, ought to be approached by means of two categories: the Spanish-language one, and its counterpart in English. Let's start with the first. In the first decade of the 21st century there were more than 700 Spanish-language radio stations in the United States, from urban centers like Los Angeles, San Antonio, Dallas,

Houston, Chicago, Miami, Tallahassee, and New York, to rural areas from coast to coast. In fact, there were more Spanish-language radio stations in the state of California than in all of Central America. These stations were oriented toward news, sports, and entertainment. A series of corporations like Radio Unica, the Hispanic Broadcasting Corporation, Entravisión, and the Spanish Broadcasting System owned most of them. A number of important personalities, like El Cucú, were listeners' favorites. The capacity of this media to mobilize audiences was tangible in the immigration marches of March 1, 2006. Today English-language radio targeting Latinos is less sizable but equally important. Programs like *Latino USA* on National Public Radio concentrate on politics and culture. Reporters like Ray Suarez and María Hinojosa, who also appear on TV, have been leading newscasters. Their unquestionable ancestor is Rubén Salazar.

### Who was Rubén Salazar?

Rubén Salazar was a journalist for the *Los Angeles Times* during the civil rights era. He refused to accept the newspaper's policy of ignoring and misrepresenting Latinos—Mexican Americans, in particular—while also pushing for a larger, more balanced ethnic representation in the American media. In that sense, he is a visionary whose contribution opened up the profession to a more diverse, less monolithic perspective of American society.

He was born in Ciudad Juárez, Mexico, on March 3, 1928. As a child he lived in Texas. He joined the army in the early 1950s and eventually got his B.A. from the University of Texas. He then worked for the *El Paso Herald Post* and later on for a Santa Rosa paper, the *The Press Democrat*. His experience was in both print and television. For the *Times* he covered the Vietnam War and was the Mexico City bureau chief correspondent, becoming the first Mexican American ever to have such a role in any American newspaper.

Speaking both English and Spanish and with a vast knowledge of the community, he was able to cover the Chicano movement in a way that satisfied the community. But he also attracted the attention of the FBI, which perceived him as a threat. His sometimes explosive language made the newspaper uncomfortable, so its management asked him to tone it down. In 1969, he became the news director of KMEX, a Spanish-language TV station, while also writing for the *Times*. Through the two venues he was able to reach a large portion of the Los Angeles population.

### How did Salazar die?

He was killed during a 1970 march in Los Angeles organized by the National Chicano Moratorium Committee, during which some 30,000 protesters walked from Belvedere Park to Laguna Park. The circumstances remain unresolved. Salazar entered a café on Whittier Boulevard. A Los Angeles Sheriff's Department officer by the name of Tom Wilson also stepped in and fired a tear-gas grenade launcher, hitting Salazar in the head with a 10-inch gas canister. The killing was ruled a homicide but Wilson was never prosecuted. Was Salazar killed because of his prominent voice in the media? Was it an accident? There is a famous oil painting at the Smithsonian American Art Museum in Washington, DC, by Frank Romero, called *The Death of Rubén Salazar* (1986), memorializing his demise. The Santa Rosa Public Library is named after him. By and large, he has become an emblem of resistance.

Salazar's journalistic involvement in the Chicano movement brought a fresh, informed perspective to the upheaval. It also broadened its scope. In that spirit, it is important to reiterate that *el movimiento*, while based within the United Farm Workers, was a larger social phenomenon. And it didn't involve Mexican Americans alone. Puerto Ricans—like the Young Lords—and Filipinos were also active.

## What are the varieties of Latino folklore?

The term "folklore" was coined by William Thoms, who defined it as "the manners, customs, observances, superstitions, ballads, proverbs, &c. of the olden time." To a large extent, these activities are a manifestation of the collective psyche. As generations come and go, they acquire a consistency that, ultimately, allows for an understanding of a people's characters. With the multiplicity of backgrounds at the heart of the Latino minority in the United States, these activities differ across national, class, and racial lines. *Quinceañera* parties, in which 15-year-old Mexican American girls celebrate their coming of age, and Cinco de Mayo parades become rich displays of folklore. Also, humor among Dominican Americans has unique characteristics, as does its counterpart among Nicaraguan Americans. Likewise, someone from a working-class background will nurture a set of beliefs different from a bourgeois person.

## Who are the most important ethnographers?

Américo Paredes, who taught at the University of Texas at Austin for years, spent his career studying, among other issues, the border *corrido*. His book *With His Pistol in His Hand: A Border Ballad and Its Hero* (1958), about the turn-of-the-19th-century border outlaw Gregorio Cortez, is one of the most significant contributions to American folklore in any ethnic group. Personally, I am fond of this book. He stands as an exemplary case of the universality that is possible to achieve through ethnography. His narrative skills offer insight into the historical, geographic, religious, legal, artistic, and personal plight of those living on the US-Mexico border. And Lydia Cabrera, a Cuban émigré who left her home as a result of Fidel Castro's Communist revolution and lived in Florida for years, devoted her attention to understanding black music, storytelling, religion, and politics in Cuba. Her book *El Monte*, loosely translated as *The Forest* and published in 1954, is an essential resource in the understanding and practice of Santería.

Interestingly, the two of them were rather unconventional ethnographers. Paredes also wrote fiction—he is the author of *The Hammon and the Beans* (1994) and *Uncle Remus con Chile* (1993)—and understood well the two sides of the creative process, as scholar and artist. His studies on Mexican folklore in South Texas defined a generation. Cabrera's style is even more impressionistic, perhaps even idiosyncratic. Her deep knowledge of Afro-Cuban folklore persuaded her that the best approach to its sources was open-ended and nondogmatic. Her first book, *Cuentos negros de Cuba* (1936), is a compilation of the Afro-Caribbean tales she heard as a child. These two scholars focused their attention on traditional popular culture, emphasizing the way memory is passed along from generation to generation.

There are other important ethnographers, such as Oscar Lewis, author of *The Children of Sanchez* (1961), about a poor family in the slums of Mexico City that rotates around a powerful patriarch.

### Is there a Latino literary tradition?

Latinos have produced a rich and varied literature. At the outset, in 1535, as the territories of what is today the Southwest were explored, there were Iberian explorers and chroniclers describing the landscape and aboriginal population. Eventually more poetic books, like Gaspar Pérez de Villagrá's 1610 epic *Historia de la Nueva México*, were written.

Spanish was the central literary vehicle until after the Treaty of Guadalupe Hidalgo, when English began to take hold. At first, it wasn't proto-Latinos who sparked readers' interest in Hispanic issues. The job was left to Americans like the novelist Washington Irving, who wrote on Columbus and the Alhambra, and the historian William Hickling Prescott, who published two popular histories of the conquest of the

Americas, one of Mexico in 1843, and the other of Peru in 1847. Mexican Americans began to explore their status, in Shakespeare's tongue, through the craft of María Amparo Ruíz de Burton. Her first novel, *Who Would Have Thought It?*, appeared anonymously in 1872, followed by a now-classic *The Squatter and the Don*, considered the first Mexican American novel published in English. It was released in 1881 under the authorship of "C. Loyal" in 1881.

### Who are the founding figures of fiction?

José Antonio Villarreal published a *bildungsroman* about adolescent adaptation called *Pocho* (1959). Richard Vásquez came out with another one called *Chicano* in 1970. Among earlier representatives are Felipe Alfau, probably the most emblematic of all, Tomás Rivera, Rudolfo Anaya, and Rolando Hinojosa.

### Who was Felipe Alfau?

The odyssey of this Barcelona-born American author is useful for understanding the publishing dilemmas faced by Latinos in the 1920s. Alfau immigrated to the United Status with his family before the Spanish Civil War. For a while he wrote music criticism for *La Prensa*, a predecessor of the merged *El Diario/La Prensa*.

Then he embraced the dream of becoming a writer and committed himself to writing a novel. He felt the market in Spanish was a dead end, so he switched to English. His novel *Locos: A Comedy of Gestures* was finished in 1928, but he was unable to sell it until almost a decade later. It was published by Farrar & Rinehart in 1936. It is a proto-postmodernist exercise along the lines of the work of Jorge Luis Borges, Vladimir Nabokov, and Luigi Pirandello, although at the time, with the exception of the latter, these authors each had yet to write their magnum opus and make an imprint in international letters. Switching to English made sense for Alfau because the immigrant Latino community in New York where he lived wasn't interested in the types of avant-garde explorations he was obsessed with.

In any case, the novel was well received but lacked a context in which to be read. And so it quickly went out of print. Then, in 1988, it was rediscovered by Dalkey Archive Press, a small publisher in Normal, Illinois, and became a classic. Alfau wrote another book in English, *Chromos* (1990), but was unable to find a publisher. He also wrote poetry. Had Alfau stayed behind and survived the Spanish Civil War, it is possible that his career would have taken a dramatically different turn. Writing books in Spanish in the United States limited his aesthetic and intellectual scope. Yet choosing English put him in a difficult situation, as it wasn't his native tongue. He wasn't part of the New York scene per se. As a result, his literature took the perspective of an outsider looking in.

### What are the Latino literary classics?

Among the most distinguished Latino writers are Sandra Cisneros (*The House on Mango Street* [1984]), Oscar Hijuelos (*The Mambo Kings Play Songs of Love* [1989]), Julia Alvarez (*How the Garcia Girls Lost Their Accent* [1991]), Cristina García (*Dreaming in Cuban* [1992]), and Junot Díaz (*Drown* [1996], *The Brief Wondrous Life of Oscar Wao* [2007], and *This Is How You Lose Her* [2012]). Their most significant works appeared in the late 1980s and throughout the 1990s, a period of fermentation for Latino art.

### What makes Junot Díaz a trailblazer?

His oeuvre, a crossover embraced not only by Latinos but also by mainstream readers in general, reflects the immigrant experience in universal ways and without apology. His characters are fully drawn. He incorporates Spanglish in a jazzy fashion. And he embraces so-called genre literature, such as comics, fantasy, and science fiction.

## What about poetry?

William Carlos Williams is a cornerstone. Born in Rutherford, New Jersey, in 1883 (and where he died at the age of 79), he was a doctor, poet, and essayist who gave a nativist twist to romanticism and modernism. His imagist poetry, his left-wing politics (he was appointed a poet laureate consultant for the Library of Congress but the job was denied to him because of his association with Communism), and his probing explorations of American history in volumes like *In the American Grain* (1925) and in his *Autobiography of William Carlos Williams* (1951) turned him into an inspiration for the Beat Generation, particularly Allen Ginsberg. There is a long-standing controversy within Latino intellectual circles regarding his own full acknowledgment of his Hispanic ancestry. (His father was Anglo and his mother Puerto Rican.)

Also a founding figure, Julia de Burgos was born in Carolina, Puerto Rico, in 1914, and she died in New York City in 1953. Her lyrical poetry plays with sexual, historical, geographical, and emotional images in a lucid, provocative fashion. She suffered from alcoholism and depression. Her famous poem "Farewell in Welfare Island" was written in 1953 while in the hospital.

## Who are their successors?

Their successors are the poets of the Chicano movement and its aftermath (Alurista, Lorna Dee Cervantes, Gary Soto), as well as Nuyorican Poets Café, a movement that came about in New York in the 1970s around the figures of Miguel Piñero and Miguel Algarín and that sought to make poetry of street life. Other Nuyorrican poets are Tato Laviera, Sandra María Esteves, Lucky Cienfuegos, and Bimbo Rivas. In 1994 Algarín and Bob Holman edited a volume called *Aloud,* sampling the origins of this artistic movement but also relating it to slam and hip-hop poetry in general.

The first Latino to become US Poet Laureate was Juan Felipe Herrera, author of *Border-Crosser with a Lamborghini Dream* (1999), *187 Reasons Mexicanos Can't Cross the Border: Undocuments 1971–2007* (2008), and *Half of the World in Light: New and Selected Poems* (2008). He was named to the post in 2015 by Librarian of Congress James H. Billington.

### How about memoirs?

Ethnic literature is by definition about the tension between the individual and the environment. A favorite genre is autobiography. It explores the trials and tribulations of the immigrant in the process of acquiring a new life. There have been several important Latino memorialists, including Oscar "Zeta" Acosta, Edward Rivera, Piri Thomas, and Carlos Eire.

### Who was Oscar "Zeta" Acosta?

Acosta was a lawyer and activist whose books *The Autobiography of a Brown Buffalo* (1972) and *The Revolt of the Cockroach People* (1973) chronicle, in the "Gonzo journalism" style of Hunter S. Thompson, the plight of Chicanos in the late 1960s and the early 1970s.

Acosta adopted the *nom de guerre* "Zeta" as he came to recognize his role as a rebellious figure. Born in El Paso, Texas, on April 8, 1935, he moved with his family to Modesto, California, in 1940. Here the events of the Sleepy Lagoon Case and the Zoot Suit Riots left an imprint on his mind, even though he was still a child when they happened. He attended Oakdale Joint Union High School and then enlisted in the US Air Force. He was shipped to Panama, where he became a minister at a lepers' colony. He completed the service, was honorably discharged, tried to commit suicide in New Orleans, married in 1956, and soon after began a 10-year-long psychiatric treatment. He eventually became a lawyer and an activist and, while on the fringes on the Chicano movement because of his excessive personality, he represented important cases during the second half of the 1960s.

"Zeta" is the model for the 300-pound Samoan in Thompson's *Fear and Loathing in Las Vegas: A Savage Journey to the Heart of the American Dream* (1971). His death is surrounded by mystery. After he ran unsuccessfully for mayor of Los Angeles, he traveled to the coastal town of Mazatlán, apparently in search of a quiet place to write. He might have been involved in the drug trade. His son received a phone call in which "Zeta" announced he was swimming in a bed of powder. He was never heard from again. Rumors about his disappearance remain unabated. There is a mythical version claiming he is still around, hidden somewhere, and plotting a takeover of the US government along with other Latin American guerrilla fighters such as Emiliano Zapata and Ernesto "Ché" Guevara.

His story has been retold in novels by the detective-fiction writers Manuel Ramos and Lucha Corpi, in a PBS documentary, and in the biography *Bandido: The Death and Resurrection of Oscar "Zeta" Acosta* (1995).

### What are the favorite genres?

The most favored genres are fiction and poetry, unquestionably. The essay as a literary form pales in comparison. There is a stereotype about Latinos being inveterate dreamers. When one thinks about the literature from south of the border, what comes to mind fast is Magic Realism, a trend, popular in the 1960s, juxtaposing dreams and reality. The most popular novel in the tradition is Gabriel García Márquez's *One Hundred Years of Solitude* (1967). Other authors, including Jorge Luis Borges, Julio Cortázar, Carlos Fuentes, and Isabel Allende, also belong to this trend. Critical thinking, on the other hand, is less popular, although not necessarily less frequent. And that is what the essay does: think critically, from an individual perspective. There have been, no doubt, important practitioners of the essay as genre in the Spanish-speaking Americas, from the before-mentioned José Enrique Rodó in Uruguay to Octavio Paz in Mexico. In the United States, the number is minuscule.

To thrive, democracy needs to be a marketplace of ideas, be they aesthetic, political, educational, or ethical. The debate of ideas shows the degree to which a society is engaged with itself and understands its mission. Fiction is an imaginative reflection of one's surroundings. Poetry is about individual insight. But the essay is a different type of tool: it ponders, it debates, it analyzes, and it digests. It elevates criticism to a civic responsibility.

### How has literature represented the Cuban exile?

There are many Cuban novels, essays, stories, plays, and poems. They include works by Guillermo Cabrera Infante, Heberto Padilla, Reinaldo Arenas, and Zoé Valdés. Symbolically, a poem by José Martí, written in exile, called "Dos patrias" uses the image of a widow to lament the fracture at the heart of the Cuban population, divided by the injury of exile. The poem opens with the following lines: "Dos patrias tengo yo: Cuba y la noche." In English: I have two homelands: Cuba and the night." Near the end of his life, Martí stated, "It is my duty to prevent, by search for Cuba's independence, the United States from spreading over the West Indies and falling, with added weight, upon other lands of Our America. All I have done up to now, and shall do hereafter, I do to that end. . . . . I have lived inside the monster and know its entrails, and my weapon is only David's slingshot."

### When did the field of Latino Studies emerge?

The field is rather recent. Or else, it should be seen as a consolidation of divergent lines of inquiry.

Since the civil rights era, a series of programs have been established in institutions of higher learning devoted to Latino studies. These programs have evolved over time. Initially they were geographically defined, focusing on national backgrounds: Chicano courses flourished in the Southwest, Cuban American courses in Florida, and Puerto Rican courses in New York. Since the 1990s the drive has been to have a broader, more encompassing scope.

These programs take a multidisciplinary approach. Their rationale is that the Latino experience needs to be understood through myriad perspectives, from anthropology to history, from sociology to literature. The flourishing of criticism has taken place within this context, sometimes at the expense of a discourse outside the academy, which is dangerous. The audience is limited to specialists and the jargon might be esoteric. In a healthy society, serious, engaging criticism—understood as a marketplace of ideas—manifests itself in a variety of forums, from the TV screen to the pulpit, from the classroom to the newspaper page.

### What about the Spanish-language book industry?

Print houses have been active in different urban centers (New York, Albuquerque, San Antonio) since before the Treaty of Guadalupe Hidalgo was signed. Although the Spanish crown had ordered public education for the native population in 1793, there was no such effort until well into the 19th century. It is known that California and New Mexico had printing presses in 1834. Authors like Juan B. Hijar y Jaro, José Rómulo Ribera, J. M. Vigil, Luis A. Torres, and by more important figures like the Chacón siblings, Eusebio (author of *Hijo de la tempestad* [1892]) and his brother Felipe Maximiliano, probed into the Mexican American experience in their oeuvre. By the end of the century there were also works written in Spanish in the United States by Cuban and Puerto Rican exiles and refugees including Eugenio María de Hostos, Lola Rodríguez de Tió, and Sotero Figueroa.

## Did the Spanish-language publishing industry change with the Chicano Movement?

An offspring of *el movimiento* were a number of ethnic publishing houses, among them Arte Público Press and Bilingual Press/Editorial Bilingüe. Interestingly, these and other publishers of Spanish-language books that were formed in the aftermath of the civil rights era initially started as magazine ventures. It was unanimously recognized by members of the Latino minority that Latinos lacked intellectual outlets through which to reflect on their history and identity.

The name of Arte Público, which launched in 1979, is reminiscent of—and even a tribute to—a federally funded publishing effort founded in Mexico in the 1920s and still active today, known as Fondo de Cultura Económica. It started in Gary, Indiana, and then moved to the University of Houston. Among its biggest sellers is Tomás Rivera's migrant classic . . . *y no se lo tragó la tierra/. . . and the Earth Did Not Devour Him* (1971), considered to be the most influential novel by a Chicano published in the second half of the 20th century. Founded in 1973, Bilingual Press published English, Spanish, and bilingual books. It publishes literary works, scholarship, and art books by or about Latinos.

## Are there more small presses?

There are several others smaller in size. These include Tonatiuh-Quinto Sol (known for its acronym TQS), originally called Quinto Sol Publications. Based in Berkeley, California, TQS was in charge of organizing literary contests to encourage Chicanos to write. The editor-in-chief was Octavio Ignacio Romano, a professor of public health at the University of California at Berkeley, who died in 2005. He edited a significant anthology of the Chicano movement, *El espejo/The Mirror*. He launched TQS in 1965. The publisher originally had an important Chicano prize, Premio Quinto Sol, which awarded $1,000 plus publication. Among the titles awarded the prize was the classic *Bless Me, Ultima* by Rudolfo Anaya, released in 1972. TQS also published other books by Anaya, including *The Legend of la Llorona* (1984).

There is also the Latin American Literary Review Press, published by Yvette Miller in Pittsburgh. It was originally launched in 1980 as a scholarly magazine, *Latin American Literary Review*, but the house has been devoted to bringing out editions of Spanish-language classics and literature of merit from across the Rio Grande. It focuses primarily on English translations of creative writing and literary criticism and poetry books, published in bilingual format.

### Which are the most censored books by Latino authors in the United States in the 21st century?

The German poet Heinrich Heine said once that where books are burned, sooner or later people are burned as well. Burning might be a literal action but it may also be a metaphor. Censorship is not only about burning but about prohibiting. That prohibition comes from an array of reasons, intolerance the source of all of them. Intolerance for difference. Democracy, of course, is built on tolerance: the ability to accept ideas that are different to ours. The opposite of tolerance is fanaticism, which George Santayana defined once as the redoubling of one's efforts when you've forgotten your objective. There are a number of Latino authors whose books often challenge the ideas accepted by the status quo in the 21st century. They include Rudolfo Anaya, Luis J. Rodriguez, Jimmy Santiago Baca, Luis Alberto Urrea, and Ariel Dorfman. Of course, there is one thing just as bad as censoring a book and that is not reading it.

### Do Latinos excel at sports?

The mystique surrounding Latino sports is universal. Watching athletes is not only a favorite pastime; it is also a palliative in times of misery. People are considerably less interested in the outcome of an election than in the final score of an important match. Soccer is a de rigueur entertainment among Spanish-speaking immigrants from Mexico to Argentina. Not surprisingly, US soccer teams showcase numerous Latino players, some imported from Latin America but the majority bred in the United States. Baseball is popular in the countries with a coast on the Caribbean Ocean, from the Dominican Republic to Venezuela, Colombia, and Panama. The Major Leagues have a multitude of Latino legends, starting with Roberto Clemente. And then there is tennis, dogfights and bullfighting, car racing, volleyball, and fencing. The tradition of Latino sports harkens back to pre-Columbian times.

### What kinds of sports are popular in Latin America?

The history of team sports in the region is defined by its colonial past. Soccer, known by the Anglicized word *el fútbol* and its less popular equivalent *el balonpié*, is the region's pastime. It is said that two entertainments capture all the attention of Spanish-language speakers: soccer and soap operas. In nations with unstable regimes and arduous economies, governments often invest in these two pastimes to distract people from more urgent problems.

Soccer is quintessential from Argentina and Brazil to El Salvador, Guatemala, and Mexico. Its place in the Caribbean Basin is minimal. Instead, *el beisbol*, also known as *el juego de pelota*, has stood as the favorite in the Dominican Republic, Cuba, and Puerto Rico since the mid-19th century, as well as in Panama and the coastal regions of Venezuela and Colombia. Historians believe that the game came to some of these countries—Nicaragua, for instance—when the US military invaded them. Apparently in Mexico, where baseball players also are important, American troops played during the 1847 invasion that was part of the Mexican-American War. In that sense, the activity is proof of the American hegemony in the hemisphere. It is believed that a returning student brought a bat and ball to Cuba in 1864.

Other athletic endeavors, such as boxing, volleyball, tennis, bullfighting and cock fighting, auto racing and horse racing, are also significant.

### Were there pre-Columbian sports?

When the Spanish conquistadors and missionaries arrived, they found a diverse, multifaceted civilization in good physical condition. Religion, politics, and the military were not the only fundamental aspects of life—so were athletics. There was one sport in particular, known as Tlachili, that was immensely popular.

In Mesoamerica, a region that goes from Mexico and Guatemala to Belize and Honduras, a sophisticated ball game with religious implications was played with a bouncing rubber ball on a stone court. Losers were sacrificed to the deities, their heads decapitated and their blood spilled over the ground, while winners would be celebrated. The game, still played for tourist recreation in the Mexican states of Yucatán and Quintana Roo, spread to El Salvador to the south and to the American Southwest to the north. It was played by the Olmecs, Maya, Zapotecs, Toltecs, and Aztecs in a stadium in front of spectators. Athletes wore gear in order to protect themselves from their opponents and from the friction with the field's stone. Because rubber wasn't known in Europe, Hernán Cortés and his soldiers were mesmerized by the ball used in the game, believing it had magical powers. Eventually they took samples back to Spain. The game was perceived to be a battle between the forces of the sun and the forces of the moon. A match would be preceded by acrobats, dancers, and other performers, as well as by musicians with flutes, whistles, trumpets, and drums.

Fittingly, Fray Diego Durán, one of the chroniclers of the age of colonization in Latin America, once said, "The man who sent the ball through the stone ring was surrounded by all. They honored him, sang songs of praise to him, and joined him in dancing. He was given a very special award of feathers or mantles and breechcloths, something very highly prized. But what he most prized was the honor involved: that was his great wealth. For he was honored as a man who had vanquished many and had won a battle." This sums up the vision of sports in Hispanic society.

### Is soccer relevant to Latinos in the United States?

The argument has been made that the emergence of soccer as a sport of national proportions is due in large part to the social rooting of Latinos in American society. Within the United States the growth of *el fútbol* is relatively recent.

Whereas in the streets of Buenos Aires children have played soccer since the early days of the 20th century, the American Youth Soccer Organization wasn't formed until 1964. In the 1970s and 1980s organizers and entrepreneurs sought to inject vitality into the sport by establishing the North American Soccer League and hiring, with expensive contracts, international stars such as Carlos Alberto and Marinho from Brazil, and Roberto Cabañas and Julio Cesar Romero from Paraguay. But it wasn't until the 1990s, when the US team started to perform well in the World Cup and women embraced the sport as well at the professional level, that a culture around it set roots. It is a known fact that immigrants and second- and third-generation Latinos are avid soccer fans and attend American stadiums with regularity, although they still prefer to follow south-of-the-border teams, especially those from their places of origin. Proof of this interest can be seen in the televised matches broadcast in Spanish on Univision and Telemundo. Likewise, Major League Soccer (MLS) organizes special matches during Hispanic Heritage Month, making available appropriate ethnic food.

Since the turn of the century, there has been an effort to vitalize MLS by pouring money into the various teams. One strategy has been to bring older European players, whose careers are on the decline, to spend their last years in the United States. Concurrently, the coaches Bruce Arena and Jürgen Klinsmann have, with a number of Latino players, pushed teams toward better international performances. Yet this performance lags behind what women's soccer has achieved at the global stage, including the World Cup. Far fewer Latino players are on the women's national teams.

### How are sports covered in Spanish-language media?

Arguably, the sports pages of newspapers like *La Opinión* in Los Angeles, *El Nuevo Herald* in Miami, *La Raza* in Chicago, and *El Diario* in New York are the sections attracting a wide readership. The same goes for channels like Fox News en Español and programs such as *República Deportiva* on Univision. One might even argue that, like few other factors, sports create an identity for Latinos in the United States. The fact that Latinos from different national origins might embrace an athlete because of his background enables the minority to build internal bridges. Ideological differences might be forgotten, even erased in an athletic match. Add to this the fact that Spanish-language broadcasters have an idiosyncratic, humorous way of delivering the news—the famous "Gooooooooooooooooal!" comes to mind—and what one gets is a distinct culture.

### Since when are Latinos visible in the Major Leagues?

Just as black players have dominated basketball for decades, Latino baseball players have multiplied in the Major Leagues. A vast number come from impoverished countries. Becoming a Major League player is a way to escape dismal conditions but also provide an economic incentive and resource for family, friends, and acquaintances. In countries like the Dominican

Republic, players like Manny Ramírez and David Ortíz become not only role models but also iconic figures.

### When did Latinos enter the Major Leagues?

No Latino equivalent to the Negro League was ever established in the United States. This is because leagues in Venezuela, Cuba, Puerto Rico, the Dominican Republic, and Cuba have been active, to some degree, since the late 19th century.

The color barrier was broken in 1947. The first dark-skinned Cuban was Orestes "Minnie" Miñoso, who played for Cleveland in 1949. The first modern-day Dominican player was Osvaldo "Ozzie" Virgil. Among the biggest stars in baseball in general, and surely among Latinos, is Roberto Clemente, originally from Puerto Rico. He played with the Pittsburgh Pirates and was the first Latino to reach the record of 3,000 hits. Clemente was active in philanthropic causes, speaking out for the poor and underrepresented. He died tragically in an airplane crash on New Year's Eve, 1972.

By the beginning of the 21st century, the roster of Latino players in just about every Major League team was astonishing, reaching at times 40%.

The passion for baseball among Latinos and the increasing number of Hispanic players always seem to be on the rise. Attendance at ballparks by Latinos is high. Teams recognize this enthusiasm by catering Spanish-language events.

### What other sports are popular?

Latinos excel in other athletic endeavors, from golf and swimming to tennis and wrestling, especially *lucha libre*.

### Is tennis played by everyone?

Tennis is, for the most part, a sport of the upper middle class. Players like Pancho Segura, Mary Joe Fernández, and Richard "Pancho" Gonzáles have excelled in it.

## And wrestling?

Latinos take a common interest in standard wrestling, whose origin is Sumerian. However, there is an idiosyncratic variety of wrestling known as *lucha libre*. Wrestlers usually wear a mask that covers their entire face, with the exception of their eyes and mouth. The purpose of the match is not only to outpower one's opponent but to unmask him too. In Mexico, where the sport is immensely popular, the act of unmasking political figures played an important role during the years when the ruling Partido Revolucionario Institucional was in control, from 1929 to 2000. Every six years, as the presidential campaign got started, the ruling leader unmasked his successor, thus establishing who would carry the mantle onward. Similarly, rebel leaders like Subcomandante Marcos, in order to protect their identity, have used a mask in public. The act of revealing their identity has been seen as a form of unmasking. The *lucha libre* folklore includes Robin Hood–like urban heroes living in working-class neighborhoods like Tepito and Nezahualcóyotl in Mexico City. They devote themselves to protecting the poor against abuse by the authorities. They include icons like El Santo, whose wrestling career, thanks to B-movies and comic strips, spread out into veritable urban myths. Their legendary status is also palpable among Mexican Americans, where passion for *lucha libre* is equally strong. The children's cartoon show on TV called *Mucha Lucha* benefits from that passion.

## What about bullfighting?

Bullfighting appears in the novels of Ernest Hemingway, significantly in *Death in the Afternoon*. It is less frequently practiced among Latinos, in spite of the strong presence the sport has south of the border. The rodeo, on the other hand, is quite popular in the Southwest, with national tournaments in cities like Las Vegas. The sport traces its roots to the colonial period. Much of the terminology used in it—words like *laso, reata, vaquero,* and *rancho*—comes from Spanish.

### How about other types of games?

Aztecs had a board game called Patolli, which is similar to backgammon. But Latinos today engage in board games that are popular south of the Rio Grande, such as *Serptientes y escaleras* and, especially, *Lotería*, a type of bingo using images of popular culture. Children have piñatas at birthday parties. Street games include *rayuela*, which is played much like hopscotch; *escondidillas*, a form of hide-and-seek; and *toma todo*, which uses a six-sided top and is not only for children but for adults too.

# 7

# WORDS AND POWER

*Are Latinos contemporaries of the rest of America?*

Power is always about the control of resources. In the 21st century, an essential resource is information. Information isn't knowledge. Knowledge is the capacity to digest—to personalize—information. That capacity, first and foremost, is the result of school. It is also a by-product of the way every one of us approaches culture. If mainstream culture is deliberately made to feel alien, the sense of alienation is substantial. To have access, one needs to have the right tools, which, in the United States, starts with a fluency in the English language. An even more proficient tool comes from knowledge of two or more languages. That is why I advocate multilingualism: in the age of globalism, it allows the speaker to have several entry doors to culture.

*What are the characteristics that make a Latino teacher?*

I don't know how to answer the question. I don't believe Latino teachers are different from anyone else. What they have different is their capacity to understand the plight of Latino students because they themselves are likely to have gone through a similar odyssey.

I am against thinking that Latino teachers should be the ones teaching Latino topics. That amounts to ghettoization. Everyone, no matter his or her background, should teach any subject as long as it is of interest.

Yet it is important that Latino teachers of grades K–12 and beyond actively advocate for an expansion of the school curriculum. Not only are they at the frontlines but they are likely to be sensitive to gaps in the textbook narrative.

I have been a teacher most of my life. I didn't set out to become one. The opportunity arose at one point and I took it. Today I can't imagine myself doing anything else with my time. Spending hours in front of young people—the teacher is the only one who ages in the classroom—allows me to keep in touch with the current trends in society.

Teaching exposes you to a whole gamut of human emotions. My Latino heritage comes across every time I'm in the classroom.

### Is the American classroom a welcoming place for Latinos?

The foremost tool of assimilation is education. Children learn, in schools, the basic principles of American life. The classroom itself is a fluid space. It needs to remain open to the changes in society. While more Latinos attend public schools than white children do, these schools can be alienating places for Latino students. This feeling results from the fact that Latino history is not reflected in the curriculum. Also, the number of Latino teachers and administrators remains small in the vast majority of districts, with the exception of areas heavily populated by Spanish speakers. There will come a time when the need to incorporate Latinos to positions of power and to make their culture an integral class component shouldn't be a nationwide effort. It is also crucial for non-Latinos to understand the Latino idiosyncrasy.

## What are the foremost challenges?

The most significant challenges are segregation, mediocre schools, low attendance, high dropout rates, the absence of appropriate Latino themes in textbooks, and a lukewarm effort to train Latino teachers. To make sure the road to citizenship is open, these challenges need to change quickly. Otherwise we are witnessing the consolidation of an underclass whose impact will be profound nationwide.

## Do Latinos learn in a different way?

The question is at the heart of multiculturalism. There is a debate that connects biology to epistemology. In other words, do Asian, black, Latino, and other minorities apprehend the world and process knowledge in ways different from the white majority? Are there genetic traits encoded in the DNA of each culture? After decades of being discredited after the egregious—and tragic—misuse that Nazism made of it during World War II, genetics is making a comeback in scientific circles. Our potential is mapped out in the cells we are constituted with, yet education, history, and chance define the path we ultimately take in life. Different ethnic groups have predispositions. Do those predispositions represent a prison of sorts? Even though they determine us, there is always room for freedom. Take interpretation: in a humanities class, a Latino student understands the material presented through the lenses of her culture. The responsibility of the teacher is to broaden that perspective, to encourage a perception of things from outside our ethnic realm.

## Should there be preferential treatment for these minorities?

Other immigrant groups have successfully gone through the American school system, and Latinos, like other ethnic minorities, deserve to be treated equally and not be given a special ride. Students learn to cope with the environment in the classroom, to identify their individual talents, to build defenses. However, since World War II the United States has undergone a demographic explosion and the mainstream culture itself is changing too. This is no longer a nation in black and white. The racial dichotomy that defined the civil rights era has been superseded by a diverse, multicultural population, one in all shades and colors. Textbooks and audiovisual materials still talk about whites first and then the rest of the population. Yes, every student should be treated as equal. Still, it is the teacher's duty to be educated too, to learn that ethnicity defines character and, thus, that ethnicity is a factor in the classroom.

### How does bilingualism define the education of Latinos?

Bilingualism is not a recent phenomenon in the United States. It has been a feature since even before the formation of the republic. Through parochial schools, immigrant communities have stressed their native language while learning English as a means to assimilate. As a federally funded effort targeting Spanish speakers, bilingual education began in Florida among Cuban exiles waiting for the downfall of Fidel Castro. In a short span of time, the program acquired stamina, transforming itself from a regional to a national program. In 1968, Title VII of the Elementary and Secondary Education Act, commonly known as the Bilingual Education Act, was passed. Its basic premise is that nonnative immigrant children are entitled to schooling in their original language while they acquire English. This means that subjects like mathematics, geography, and social sciences are taught in Spanish by teachers fluent in the language. When the child is finally able to learn in English, they move into the general classroom.

Upon their arrival to the United States, some immigrant children have only a partial knowledge of Spanish and none of English. In such cases the bilingual education program is needed so that they first can use their original tongue as a learning tool. Immigrant parents are not always aware of the choices available for their children. Plus, issues like race and class played a major role in the success of the program. In affluent neighborhoods where first-rate teachers are available and technological and other resources are not scarce, learning English isn't necessarily an obstacle. This is often the case where whites live. Things are more difficult in the inner city and in remote rural schools, where fine teachers are hard to find, classrooms are ill equipped, and the rationale for swiftly moving students from Spanish to English lessons is confused.

### Was Bilingual Education successful?

Advocates believed the program was a more humane strategy in the process of assimilation for newcomers. It allows families to keep in touch with their culture while becoming American. Critics point to the same elements as signs of disaster. They want English to be the only language taught in public schools, suggesting that teaching children Spanish results in a dual loyalty and handicaps them on the road to enjoying all the benefits the United States offers to immigrants. Thus, in the last years of the 20th century and the first of the 21st, a movement to debunk bilingual education was orchestrated in a number of states. Resolutions to stop federal funding were passed in California (1998), Arizona (2000), and Massachusetts (2002). The alternative was a program known as English immersion, also known as sink-or-swim, in which students were directly placed in classrooms where English was exclusively used.

### Are there similar programs for other minorities?

While bilingual education was perceived to be targeted exclusively for Latinos, Asian Americans (Chinese, Korean, Vietnamese, Cambodians, etc.) also benefited from it.

### Why are Latinos underrepresented in higher education?

Enrollment numbers are dangerously low. In the Northeast, where the elite institutions are concentrated, the percentages are scandalous: at places like Harvard, Brown, Columbia, Yale, Amherst, and Williams, the Latino student body averages 7%. These places remain a bastion of elitist white power. Unless they open up, fundamental aspects of society won't change.

### Is activism a common path for Latino students in higher education?

The civil rights era left a lasting legacy. Students in Prague, Czech Republic; Paris, France; Mexico City; and Berkeley, California, protested vocally, marched on the street, and took over buildings. It was an age of dissent. A slogan painted on a Paris wall might be used to define the entire generation: "Be realistic, demand the impossible." Chicanos and Puerto Ricans were defined by the period and their vision continues into the present. There is a loyalty to activism among ethnic students in general and among Latinos in particular. It results from decades of frustration and connects with a tradition of rebellion in Latin America dating back to the colonial period. Think of Fray Bartolomé de Las Casas, Enriquillo, Sor Juana Inés de La Cruz, Ernesto "Ché" Guevara, and Subcomandante Marcos. Still, the transformation of the curriculum is likely to happen not through violence but patience. Change needs to come from internal committees inside the institutions.

### Are there teachers who have become role models?

At the college level there are intellectuals whose careers have opened unexplored paths. Pedro Henríquez Ureña, a scholar from the Dominican Republic with a doctorate from the University of Minnesota, expanded the debate on Hispanic culture through essays on history, language, and literature.

He delivered the Charles Eliot Norton Lectures at Harvard University in 1940–1941. They were published under the title *Literary Currents in Hispanic America* in 1945. His sister, Camila Henríquez Ureña, taught at Vassar College. And their brother, Max, a year younger than Pedro, was a specialist in the literary movement called *Modernismo*. Ernesto Galarza, a pioneering Chicano scholar and militant for labor rights, who was born in 1905 in Puerto Vallarta, Mexico, and died in 1984 in San Jose, California, authored scores of articles and several books on Latin American and Latino history, labor, and agriculture, and he is famous for his memoir *Barrio Boy* (1971). These are only a few scholars. Arguably the most famous high school mathematics teacher is Jaime Escalante, a Bolivian immigrant from La Paz who came to represent educational reform in California after he pushed his students, the majority of whom were portrayed as being at risk, to improve on their Advanced Placement exam in calculus in 1982. The movie *Stand and Deliver* (1988) chronicles his achievement.

### Does the word have power?

There has been a written record of the Latino experience ever since the arrival of the Spanish explorers. At first this record was in Spanish and, through poetry and plays, it reflected the dilemmas of colonialism. In the late 19th century, English-language novels began to appear, chronicling the fight for land after the Treaty of Guadalupe Hidalgo and the Gadsden Purchase. The political overtone became more intense among intellectuals as the struggle for independence and self-determination in Cuba and Puerto Rico swept the Northeast. Immigration, ghetto life, and assimilation are fixtures of a more recent ethnic mode. The dilemma of language remains as publishers in the United States, capitalizing on a polyphonic market, release books in Spanish, English, and bilingual formats. Plus, Spanglish is a literary force to reckon with.

*Moving on to the topic of words, is there*
*such a thing as purity in language?*

Purity in language is a chimera. Words and the patterns they
follow are in constant change. On the road to assimilation,
newcomers slowly give up their immigrant tongues in favor
of the equalizing English. Gaelic, Italian, German, Finnish,
Yiddish, and Polish disappeared as active modes of communication in the United States. Spanish is not necessarily doing the
same. Its stamina and usefulness are on the ascent, although
in contaminated form, reshaping its syntactical structure, and
filled with borrowings. In fact, a new language has emerged,
although it is not standardized yet: Spanglish. Judging by the
music, literature, advertising, and, in general, by its ubiquitous
use in daily life, it has more than proven to be a viable way of
communication.

A broader question emerges from this: Is it a tool or an obstacle for Latinos to become part of the American mainstream?

*Does language have larger political implications?*

The use of Spanish, once ignored in the political sphere,
has become invaluable. Since the presidential campaigns of
George H. W. Bush and Michael Dukakis, candidates, when
possible, engage in limited Spanish-language exchanges. More
importantly, increasing amounts of money are allocated by the
major parties for ads in Spanish-language TV and radio. In
the 2004 presidential campaigns of George W. Bush and John
Kerry, there was more per-voter investment in Univision and
Telemundo than in any of the major English-language channels like ABC, CBS, and NBC.

*How many people speak Spanish in the United States?*

In 2016, the number was close to 40 million. Obviously, not all
Latinos speak Spanish. In fact, the younger generation does-
n't, although, judging by the popularity of the language on

campuses nationwide, there is a broad move to reclaim it. And, of course, many non-Latinos speak Spanish as well.

The allergy the Trump administration projected toward multilingualism contributed, in early 2017, to making Spanish a sort of language of resistance. There are states like Texas, Colorado, California, Arizona, and Florida where its use is so widespread that it is considered the state's "unofficial" second tongue.

There is a branch in New York of the Real Academia Española, the Royal Academy of the Spanish Language. Founded in 1973, it is called Academia Norteamericana de la Lengua Española, and it is perceived as Eurocentric, lethargic, and disconnected from day-to-day life in the United States, to the point that its existence is almost totally unknown by the vast majority of Latinos. Its directors are all male and the average age is 60.

### Since when has Spanish been present in the United States?

While English, since prior to the birth of the republic in 1776, has served as an equalizer, other tongues have been present in the history of the United States. A plethora of aboriginal languages were spoken before the arrival of the British Pilgrims. Within a few decades of the anchoring of the *Mayflower*, in 1620, with the spread of settlements across New England, English established itself as the lingua franca of the colonies. As successive waves of immigrants made it to these shores, with their respective tongues, they gave them up to embrace the nation's common vehicle of communication.

Like Iroquois, Cherokee, and Navajo, Spanish was already a fixture of the social landscape before the *Mayflower*. It was used in missions and settlements under Iberian rule in Florida and within the territories that constitute the Southwest today. It was also influenced by Nahuatl, Mayan, and, to a lesser extent, by other pre-Columbian tongues used in New Spain, as Mexico was called in the colonial period and until its independence in 1810. However, in the late 19th century and throughout the 20th century, other forms of Spanish also established themselves in the United States. Today the varieties are plentiful: each immigrant group within the Latino minority brings with itself its own verbal idiosyncrasy. Spanish is the second most spoken language in the country.

There are major Spanish-language newspapers, such as *El Diario* in New York, *La Opinión* in Los Angeles, *La Raza* in Chicago, and *El Nuevo Herald* in Miami. Similarly, there are two Spanish-language TV networks, Univision and Telemundo, catering to an audience of millions. They are also the fastest-growing networks in the market in terms of advertising. The number of radio stations is immense and widespread. In California alone, the number of Spanish-program affiliates is larger than that of all Central American countries together. Plus, there are publishers of Spanish books for all ages.

### Is there one Spanish in Latin America or are there many?

The year 1492 is the *annus mirabilis* of Hispanic civilization. Three major events took place: Columbus's journey across the Atlantic in search of an alternative commercial route to the Indies, in response to the Turk blockade of the navigational path used in those days; the expulsion of the Jews from the Iberian Peninsula, which allowed the Catholic Queen Isabella of Castile and King Ferdinand of Aragón to make Spain an unequivocally Catholic nation; and the publication, by the Salamanca philologist Antonio de Nebrija, of the first grammar of the Spanish language. This third event is often overlooked, yet it had a gigantic historical impact. As the Spanish crown sought ways to expand its areas of influence, its language—*el español*—became a tool in the colonizing effort. The language had started as a regional dialect in Castile and competed, along with Catalan, Galician, and other dialects, all somewhat connected to the "vulgar Latin," for a stake in the imperial endeavors. But while other dialects ended up being eclipsed, Spanish became the homogenizing force, both on the peninsula and in its colonies.

### Is language a prism whereby to understand the conquest?

As Hernán Cortés, Francisco Pizarro, Pánfilo de Narváez, and other conquistadors and explorers took control of the Americas, from 1523 onward, Spanish became the principal tool of control and "civilization" of the aboriginal people. The Bible was forced upon the Indians in Spanish. And as racial mixing occurred between Spaniards and the Indians (mestizos), and between Spaniards and African slaves brought to perform hard labor (mulattos), the colonial effort made the language the hemispheric code in business transactions, politics, and religion. In time each country developed its own variety of Spanish. While all share the same grammatical rules, certain characteristics distinguish the Spanish spoken in different countries. A couple of passing instances: *vos* is used in the River Plate region (Argentina and Uruguay) for the second-person singular, and a conjugation related to *vosotros* is then adapted, as in "*¿Vos venís mañana?*" In Colombia the second-person formal address *usted* is widely used, even in intimate relations. A daughter might say to her mother, *Usted es mi madre.*

### How did Spanish replace the aboriginal tongues in the region?

The conquest of the Americas is often presented in textbooks as a military enterprise with racial, economic, sexual, and political consequences. It ought to be approached too from the linguistic viewpoint. The spread of Spanish came at the expense of dozens of aboriginal tongues. The conquistadors and missionaries thought of the natives as uncivilized, a catchword whose synonyms included barbaric, pagan, and downright inferior. Early on in intellectual circles there was debate about the humanity of aboriginal peoples. And their languages too were described as undeveloped. While this approach was widespread, there were Spanish thinkers and activists who resisted these simplifications. Other missionaries devoted themselves to codifying the pre-Columbian languages. It is thanks to them that it is possible to know their vocabulary and syntactical development. Nevertheless, theirs was a scholarly effort.

### What happened with Spanish during the colonial period?

The colonial period fermented the value of Spanish, a tongue taught to the indigenous population in missions. Such was the scale of indoctrination that by the time the independent spirit swept the Americas, from Mexico to Argentina and Colombia, no other language came even close in influence. To be educated, to have access to civil and ecclesiastical power, implied knowledge of Spanish. Conversely, to various degrees the pre-Columbian tongues were ridiculed and ostracized. Such marginalization didn't altogether succeed in some countries, allowing, for example, Guaraní to become Paraguay's de facto second language. In Bolivia, secondary languages include Inca, Quechua, and Aymara. Yet these are exceptions. It is only in the last decades of the 20th century that instruction in Nahuatl, Quechua, Maya, Zapotec, and other indigenous languages has been allowed in Mexico, Guatemala, and elsewhere.

### What is the English-Only Movement?

There are different sorts of organizations, voter initiatives, lobbying efforts, campaigns, and other efforts to fight bilingual education as a federally supported program. One of them is the English-Only movement. This movement was a response to the increase of the Latino population in states like Florida, Texas, and California. It was also a response to the 1974 decision by the Supreme Court, known as *Lau v. Nichols*, which ruled that when children arrive in schools with little or no knowledge of English, using a full English immersion program was a violation of their civil rights. The term "English-Only" was coined in 1980 in Dade County, Florida, by people who supported the ordinance prohibiting "expenditures of any county funds for the purpose of utilizing any language other than English or any culture other than that of the United States."

## What is English-First?

As a movement it has a similar premise as English-Only but is less lopsided. It argues that English should be the only legitimate language of governmental communication in the country, although it doesn't negate the existence and dissemination of other languages as long as they don't pose a serious threat to the nation's cohesiveness.

There have been initiatives and referendums in various metropolitan centers, especially those in demographic transition, to rule English as the prime vehicle of communication. Some of these have passed in resounding fashion. It is important to stress that English is not referred to in the US Constitution as an "official language," even though there have been attempts—such as the English language amendment introduced in 1981 by California Senator S. I. Hayakawa—to establish it as such.

## Is English the official language of the United States?

Nowhere in the Constitution is it stated that the nation has an official language. It seems to have been clear to the Founding Fathers that the United States needed a flag, a currency, a common history, and a shared set of values but not the need to declare one language as the sole vehicle of communication. The concept, it seemed to them, infringed on the First Amendment. However, over the years a series of nativist attempts at making English official have taken place.

*Have all immigrant groups had bilingual education?*

Yes, every immigrant wave, no matter the origin, has established parochial and charter schools designed to teach children English as well as the group's original language. Only in the 1960s were these efforts transformed into a federally funded program. This means that the money used to sponsor bilingual classes is paid by the taxpayers. It is only natural that those opposed to it should campaign openly to debunk the program.

*What is Spanglish?*

Spanglish is a modality of speech used on a daily basis by millions of people in the United States. The majority of users are Latino, although non-Latinos (e.g., Anglos and other ethnic minorities) engage in it too. Plus, as a result of the global influence of American culture everywhere in the world, one might also encounter it in Spain, the Caribbean Basin, and major metropolises such as Buenos Aires, Caracas, Lima, and Bogotá.

In their parlance, Spanglish speakers engage in three traceable strategies: code-switching, automatic translation, and the coining of neologisms. Code-switching is the free-flowing transit by a bilingual person from one language to another. A typical dialogue goes:

"Oye, Nicolás, wasup?"
"Notin' much. Mi vieja needs me to be en casa en la noche?"
"Po'qué?"
"Cause ella necesita salir and someone has to keep un ojo on my sister."

The bilingual person is not necessarily fluent in either Spanish or English. In fact, Spanglish is used by people with partial knowledge of their immigrant tongue, whose immersion in the English-language environment is not yet complete. Not all Spanglish speakers have a limited acquaintance with the two languages. A large number are fluent in both yet enjoy the art of code-switching, which sociolinguists have been studying in research institutions for decades.

### When does automatic translation occur?

It happens when a Spanglish speaker thinks in one language but uses another, resulting in syntax that shows signs of cross-fertilization. An example: *"Te llamo p'atrás."* The expression means literally "I'll call you back." Syntactically, it makes no sense in Cervantes' tongue. The correct expression is *"Te devuelvo la llamada,"* but people living at the crossroads of Hispanic and Anglo civilizations no longer use it. Instead, they translate the English saying word-for-word.

### What about the coining of Spanglishisms?

Spanglish speakers are prone to creating new terms: *"wáchale"* for "watch out" and *"La Migra"* for Immigration Patrol. The number of Spanglishisms in use today is enormous. Some are regional, while others are used at the national level. A handful come from adolescent lingo, sports, advertising, and the Internet, which has come to be known as Cyber-Spanglish. In 2003, a lexicon was edited with approximately 6,000 words, called *Spanglish: The Making of a New American Language.* Depending on where a Spanglish speaker might be with regards to age, nationality, and education, the sentence structure might be English-based sprinkled with Spanish terms, or vice versa.

### Is there only one Spanglish in the United States?

Because Spanglish is currently in transition from a purely oral way of communication to a codified one, it would be a mistake to describe it as a clearly defined language. It is closer to a slang, although the speed with which it is establishing its own grammatical rules is astonishing. Likewise, there is not a single, homogenized Spanglish recognizable all over the United States, let alone abroad. Instead, there is a plethora of varieties, each of which might be subdivided. Cuban Americans in Miami speak a type of Spanglish known as Cubonics. Other Cuban Americans elsewhere in the country—say Union City, New Jersey—might use a similar, though not identical form of speech. Dominican Americans in Washington Heights, New York, have developed their own linguistic way, known as Dominicanish. There is also Nuyorrican, Chicano Spanglish, Pachuco, and so on. The Spanish language arrived in the Americas with Columbus and his fleet, at the end of the 15th century. With time, each nation developed its own verbal identity. As immigrants of those nations have found their way to the United States, the different verbal identities have stamped their imprimatur on the varieties of Spanglish one is able to hear.

### What is the use of Spanglish in commerce and the media?

The dramatic growth of the Latino community in the United States since World War II is making Spanglish an unavoidable cultural reality. Other immigrant groups also engaged in code-switching and verbal invention, but since their demographic numbers were limited, these ways of communication had little impact in the mainstream. The opposite is true in the case of Spanglish. At the dawn of the 21st century, this modality seems everywhere. It is essential in businesses like construction, restaurants, health care, and the legal profession. Spanglish is often used in court houses, to an extent that the judge may be forced to order in a translator. Also, it is only necessary to step in ethnic restaurants and food kitchens to witness the extent to which the workforce communicates by code-switching. Plus, Latino students in elementary, middle, and high schools, and at the college level, use Spanglish when speaking with teachers.

### Is its use prevalent in business?

Large corporations and small companies are aware of the linguistic temperature of the country. MTV frequently uses Spanglish, and there are numerous radio stations from the Southwest to the Northeast using it partially or all the time. Companies like Mountain Dew, Taco Bell, and Hallmark showcase it. Even the US Army uses Spanglish in its recruiting ads. This embrace has helped make the parlance "cool" among people of all backgrounds. In the arts, there are already novels, short stories, and collections of poems available in it, and even a partial translation of Cervantes' masterpiece, *Don Quixote of La Mancha*. Needless to say, the most prominent artistic venue is music. For years Spanglish has been used by Latin singers in rhythms as diverse as *corridos*, salsa, *merengue, bachata*, and *reggaetón*.

### And in politics?

If something clicks in society, politicians are likely to embrace it. Spanish has been regularly used by Latino politicians since the colonial period, especially in New Mexico, Arizona, California, and Texas. In the late 19th century and throughout the 20th century, as Latinos were stereotyped negatively in the popular imagination, the language became associated with a lower class deprived of political cachet. With Latinos becoming the largest ethnic minority, this attitude is changing. And not only is Spanish being used by politicians, but it is being used at every level, from presidents like Bill Clinton to state and local figures like Bill Richardson in New Mexico, Jeb Bush in Florida, and Antonio Villaraigosa in California.

Spanglish too has been a channel to connect with the Latino electorate. In his first and second presidential campaigns, George W. Bush used his nephew, the son of Governor Jeb Bush in Florida and a fluent Spanglish speaker, to deliver speeches to Latino audiences. As a rule, the audiences were receptive to these messages and forgiving of someone whose use of the language—whether Spanish or Spanglish—is limited. On occasion these political maneuvers backfire, in particular when a politician is not aware of linguistic nuances that distinguish a variety of Spanglish from the rest.

### Are the translations of literary classics into Spanglish available?

Indeed, I translated the first chapter of *Don Quixote* in 2001. It was published in the literary supplement of the Catalan daily *La Vanguardia*. Since then I have translated the entire novel. Several other chapters have also been released. I followed this with a scene from Shakespeare's *Hamlet*, a portion from Charles Dickens's *Great Expectations*, and *El Little Príncipe* (*The Little Prince*).

Every translation is an appropriation. My love for Spanglish is immense. My renditions are an effort to make an assortment of classics available to a Spanglish-speaking audience as deserving of that literature as anyone else in other languages.

Here are two samples. First, Hamlet's soliloquy (Act 3, Scene 1):

HAMLET: Ser, or not to ser: esa es la question.
Whether 'tis nobler sufrir en la mente
The slings y flechas of outrageous fortuna,
O tomar las arms against un mar de troubles,
Y al oponerlos end them? Morir, dormir,
No more, y, by domir to say que terminamos
The heart-ache y los mil natural shoques
Que la carne is heir to 'tis a consumación
Devoutly to be deseada. Morir, dormir;
Dormir, perchance soñar: ay, there's el obstáculo:
For in that sueño of death what sueños may come
Cuando hemos shuffled off this coil mortal
Must darnos pausa. There's el respecto
That makes calamidad of una vida tan larga:

For quién puede soportar the whips and scorns del tiempo,
El opresor's wrong, the proud man's contumely,
Los pangs of dispriz'd amor, the law's retraso,
La insolencia of office, y los spurns
Que ameritan pacientemente the unworthy takes,
Cuando él mismo might his quietus make
Con a bare bodkin? who would fardels bear,
Gruñir y jurar under a weary vida,
But that the dread of algo después de la muerte,
The undiscover'd país de cuyo bourn
No viajero retorna, puzzles the will,
Y makes us rather bear esos males we have
Than fly a otros that we no conocemos?
Thus la conciencia does make cobardes de todos nosotros;
Y thus the native hue de la resolución
Is sicklied o'er con el pálido cast del pensamiento,
Y empresas de gran pith y moment
With este regard sus currents turn awry,
And lose el nombre de la acción. Soft you ahora!
The fair Ophelia! Nymph, in thy plegarias
Sean todos mis pecados remember'd.

And portions of chapter 2 of *El Little Príncipe*:

And entonces yo viví alone, con nadie con quien pudiera hablar, hasta seis años atrás cuando mi avión se descompuso en el Desierto del Sahara. Y yo no tenía un mechanic conmigo, o ningún pasajero, por lo que yo tenía que hacer un complicated arreglo de engine por mi cuenta. Mi vida depended de esto, since yo apenas tenía suficiente agua que would last me una semana.

La first noche, me acosté en el ground and me quedé asleep, millas y millas lejos de cualquier livin alma. Yo estaba más cut off que un barco adrifteando en el middle del océano. So seguramente podrás imaginarte mi astonishment cuando yo fui awekeado en el daybreak por una funny little voz que decía: "Please, puedes dibujarme un little cordero!"

"Qué!"

"Dibújame un little cordero . . ."

Pronto salté to mis pies como si hubiera sido struck by lightnin.

Me froté los ojos y miré. And ví el más extraordinario little fellow estudiándome intensamente. Esta es la mejor portrait que yo have been able to dibujar de él desde entonces.

### Is there an equivalent of the Royal Academy of the Spanish Language in Spanglish?

Happily, not yet.

# EPILOGUE: 100 ARTIFACTS

This list of objects is an anchor in understanding the history of Latinos in the United States. If I had to rewrite this book (or perhaps create a museum exhibit out of it), I would take the "object" approach. Each object would be accompanied by a 500-word caption. In terms of sequence, I have deliberately chosen an arbitrary order because, while the temptation to organize history chronologically is understandable, life itself is haphazard:

1. A *calavera* (sugar skull) for Día de los Muertos
2. The last baseball bat used by Roberto Clemente
3. The poem *"Dos patrias"* (1893) by José Martí
4. Lin-Manuel Miranda's score of the Broadway musical *In the Heights*
5. A sign that reads "No dogs or Mexicans allowed," used in California in the 1940s
6. A T-shirt with the face of "Ché" Guevara
7. A flag of the United Farm Workers
8. A "selfie" taken by a DREAMer during a protest
9. A Spanish/English dictionary
10. A *lucha libre* mask
11. A crucifix

12. A recording of the border *corrido* "The Ballad of Gregorio Cortez" (1958)
13. A still from *I Love Lucy* (1951)
14. One of Fidel Castro's cigars
15. An action figure of Sam Houston
16. A photograph of Lolita Lebrón and other Puerto Rican nationalists after they fired shots in the US House of Representatives (1954)
17. A Spanish-language translation of the *Qur'an* from the detainee library at the Guantánamo Detention Camp
18. The hat worn by Teddy Roosevelt during the Rough Riders invasion of Cuba
19. A first edition of María Amparo Ruíz de Burton's *The Squatter and the Don* (1885)
20. A Pachuco zoot suit
21. A facsimile of the Treaty of Guadalupe Hidalgo (1848)
22. The recipe for "*Moros y cristianos*"
23. A disposed Green Card
24. The *Los Angeles Times* front page with news of the Sleepy Lagoon Case (1943)
25. A copy of *The Autobiography of a Brown Buffalo* (1972), by Oscar "Zeta" Acosta
26. An altar for Selena Quintanilla
27. A "romantic" classified ad in the newspaper *La Opinión*
28. A poster of the Tin Tan movie *El rey del barrio* (1950)
29. A pair of large gold earrings
30. A *retablo*, a devotional painting using Catholic iconography
31. A beret used by the Puerto Rican Young Lords
32. An ear of corn, which reached North America from Central America around 2100 BCE
33. A copy of *El Little Príncipe* (2016), by Antoine de Saint Exupéry, translated into Spanglish
34. A bottle with potion from a Santería ritual
35. A white Guayabera, a lightweight and classy shirt used in the Caribbean

36. A flag from the Puerto Rican Day Parade in Manhattan
37. An assortment of Latino emojis
38. Lowriders paraphernalia
39. A *molcajete* containing guacamole
40. A black-and-white photo of Julia de Burgos
41. A recording of the merengue musician Juan Luis Guerra singing *"Ojalá que llueva café"* (1989)
42. A postage stamp of the math teacher Jaime Escalante
43. A miniature taco truck
44. A guitar painted with the rainbow colors
45. A poster of Celia Cruz
46. A bottle of Corona
47. The chronicle of the expedition through Florida of Alvar Nuñez Cabeza de Vaca
48. A Virgen del Cobre figurine
49. A lunchbox with images of *Dora the Explorer*
50. A portrait of a Puerto Rican soldier who fought in the Iraq War
51. A signed copy of the Jones-Shafroth Act (1920)
52. A photo of Peter O'Toole playing Don Quixote in *Man of La Mancha* (1965)
53. A playbill of *Zoot Suit* (1978), by Luis Valdéz
54. The saxophone of Paquito D'Rivera
55. A bottle of Ortega salsa, medium: Thick & Chunky
56. A hardcover copy of *My Beloved World* (2013), by Supreme Court Justice Sonia Sotomayor
57. A yuca root
58. A Reina Valera Spanish translation of the Bible (1602)
59. A menu from the Miami restaurant La Carreta
60. A set of *Lotería* cards
61. *Quinceañera* apparel
62. A can of Café Bustelo
63. The 15th-century map used by Columbus
64. A napkin from Taco Bell
65. A set of women's Tango dance shoes
66. A barbed wire from the US-Mexico border fence

67. Pro-life and pro-choice buttons
68. A Pulparindo (tamarind candy)
69. A copy of *Poems, Protest, and a Dream* (1997), by Sor Juana Inés de la Cruz
70. A gun used by the young gang Ñetas
71. Leonard Bernstein's music score of *West Side Story* (1961)
72. A video of Cantinflas's film *Allí está el detalle* (1940)
73. A parodic depiction of Pancho Villa's skull
74. A torture instrument used by the Holy Office of the Inquisition
75. An Alamo historical artifact, donated to the state of Texas by the British rock star Phil Collins
76. A Paracas textile from Peru
77. A copy of the Qur'an in a Spanish translation by Julio Cortés Soroa (1980)
78. A wooden school bench with multiple inscriptions in Spanish and English carved into it
79. A video of Louis CK talking about his Spanish roots
80. A photo of Gloria Anzaldúa
81. A photo of the frontispiece of the Milta Café in San Bernardino, California
82. A leather jacket with Speedy Gonzalez painted on the back
83. A bunch of tomatoes, which were first grown by Aztecs in Mexico, who used them in cooking around 500 CE
84. A baseball card of Dodgers pitcher Fernando Valenzuela
85. A Mariachi suit
86. A bag of M&M's with all the packaging text in Spanish
87. A copy of the *Gramática* (1492) by Antonio de Nebrija
88. Some items from the 300,000 gold seekers during the California Gold Rush
89. The census document used by the Nixon administration in which the word "Hispanic" appears for the first time
90. A TV ad for *Modern Family* (2009) with the actress Sofia Vergara
91. A poster of Carmen Miranda

92. A copy of *Green Lantern* (2013) with its heroine, Jessica Cruz
93. A cup of hot *Chocolate Abuelita*, made from cocoa beans originally used in 1000 BCE in Central America
94. A colorful *hamaca* (hammock)
95. A dollar bill with the image of George Washington wearing an Emiliano Zapata moustache
96. The painting "Tamalada" (2008) by Carmen Lomas Garza
97. A *pataconera*, used to make fried plantains
98. A photo of the actor Antonio Banderas playing *Zorro*
99. The poster of *Sun Mad Raisins* by Ester Hernández
100. A copy of *What Everyone Needs to Know: Latinos in the United States* (2018)

# AFTERWORD: WE ARE ALL DREAMERS

Not to be attuned to their fate is inhuman. Letting them be expelled from the country without resistance is a form of complicity.

The future of close to 1.3 million "Dreamers"—recipients of the program called Deferred Action for Childhood Arrivals (DACA)—is unquestionably the most consequential issue facing Latinos in the United States since the turn of the millennium.

The Dreamers are young people who were brought to the United States as infants. Their parents, given the unstable economic, social, and political scene in Mexico, Guatemala, Nicaragua, El Salvador, and other nearby countries, brought them to the United States in search of a better life. In other words, these young women and men didn't choose to come. The decision was made for them.

Amidst the heated immigration debate in Washington, Congress has never managed to pass the DREAM (Development, Relief, and Education for Alien Minors) Act, first introduced in 2001 and debated over several Congresses. In response, President Barack Obama signed an executive order in 2012 allowing Dreamers to come out of the shadows and register with the federal government in exchange for a temporary reprieve from deportation.

To be eligible, Dreamers needed to have arrived before 2007, at which time they needed to have been 15 years old or younger; to either be enrolled in high school or have a high school diploma; and to have no criminal record.

While not promoted by President Obama as a de facto amnesty, the offer was compassionate. Naturally, about 800,000 Dreamers registered.

In 2016, Donald Trump made the repeal of DACA one of the signatures of his presidential campaign. He promised to dismantle it as soon as he came to office. In September 2017, eight months into his term in the White House, he foolishly kept his promise. It was a dark day in the nation's history.

This was a way for President Trump to satisfy his angry, mostly white, base, whose rage by all accounts stemmed from having been bypassed, in the age of globalism, by predominantly younger and better-trained workers. While Trump's base rejected such accusations, this rage was racially motivated. Those benefiting from globalism were people of color. Plus menial jobs, which Trump supporters deemed unworthy, were performed predominantly by poor Latinos, a majority of them Spanish speakers.

In short, the way politicians played ping-pong with Dreamers was shameful. Many Dreamers didn't even know their legal status until applying to college. The idea of sending them back home was preposterous. Home was in the United States. This is the only country they knew. This is the only country they loved. Under DACA, they had voluntarily offered their names and personal information to the federal government in return for a humane reprieve. The Trump administration took advantage of that information to identify them in their homes, schools, and places of work.

The argument that the repeal of DACA was an affirmation of this country's law and order had no merit. It is true that the immigration system had been abused for several decades. It was broken and needed to be fixed. But blaming Dreamers for lawlessness was hypocritical. These young women and men were law-abiding citizens about to start their careers. They had abandoned the shadow of nondocumentation with the promise of a slice of the American Dream. And then they were betrayed. The fact that they were all young, still at an age when a person is shaping one's own worldview, was tragic.

Shortly after Attorney General Jeff Sessions announced the repeal of DACA on television in September 2017, giving Dreamers and Congress six months to sort out the conundrum, President Trump sent a tweet in which he seemed ambivalent about it. He said he had "a lot of love" for Dreamers and that they had "nothing to worry about for six months." He followed the tweet with an agreement made with the Democrats in which he appeared to change his mind completely, not only saying that Dreamers would be able to stay but recanting from this signature pledge to build a wall between Mexico and the United States. Among many of Trump's supporters, this position gave place to fury. Red caps with the sign "Make America Great Again" were burned in various parts of the country.

Rather than an expression of affection, the zigzagging appeared to be yet another stab in the back. One doesn't love people who are forced to be separated from their relatives and friends.

Of course, beyond the tragedy of looming deportations, the elimination of DACA represented a significant impact to the overall US economy. The total number of Dreamers is close to one sixtieth of the overall Latino population in the United States. Their income would obviously contribute to the well-being of millions of families. Furthermore, according to one estimate, ending DACA would end up costing the federal government $60 billion in tax and employment contributions. It would decrease economic growth by $280 billion over the next ten years.

Images of agents arriving with warrants to homes, classrooms, and other sites contribute to an atmosphere of anxiety. I am a teacher. I love my students dearly. Such images are disturbing. I am also a Mexican Jew. My ancestors were victims of anti-Semitism in Europe. Officers arrived in the middle of the night to take a handful of them away. The family never saw them again.

The repeal of DACA was a xenophobic outburst. It was racist. It was anti-Latino. A nation is a work in progress. It needs to be defended, from not only its enemies, but also fearmongering forces within it. Sometimes those forces are high up, in government offices. That shouldn't stop anyone from fighting for justice. The ability to protest is what makes the United States the land of freedom.

In retrospect, it seems fitting that we refer to these promising youngsters as Dreamers. The word is intrinsically linked to the American Dream. In the United States, we are all dreamers. But since an attack against one American is an attack against all, we are all Dreamers too.

—October 2nd, 2017

# FURTHER READING

Abreu, Christina D. *Rhythms of Race: Cuban Musicians and the Making of Latino New York City and Miami, 1940–1960*. Chapel Hill: University of North Carolina Press, 2015.

Aldama, Frederick, ed. *The Routledge Companion to Latina/o Popular Culture*. New York: Routledge, 2016.

Aldama, Frederick, with Christopher González, eds. *Graphic Borders: Latino Graphic Books Past, Present, and Future*. Austin: University of Texas Press, 2016.

Bayor, Ronald H., ed. *The Oxford Handbook of American Immigration and Ethnicity*. New York: Oxford University Press, 2016.

Behnken, Brian D., ed. *Civil Rights and Beyond: African American and Latino/a Activism in the Twentieth-century United States*. Athens: University of Georgia Press, 2016.

Brown, Nadia E., with Sarah Allen Gershon, eds. *Distinct Identities: Minority Women in US Politics*. New York: Routledge, 2016.

Chavez, Cesar. *An Organizer's Tale: Speeches*. Edited and with an introduction by Ilan Stavans. New York: Penguin Classics, 2008.

Colón-Muñiz, Anaida, with Magaly Lavadenz, eds. *Latino Civil Rights in Education: La Lucha Sigue*. New York: Routledge, 2016.

Coronado, Raúl. *A World Not to Come: A History of Latino Writing and Print Culture*. Cambridge, MA: Harvard University Press, 2013.

Davis Undiano, Robert Con. *Mestizos Come Home! Making and Claiming Mexican-American Identity*. Norman: University of Oklahoma Press, 2017.

Dunne, John Gregory. *Delano: The Story of the California Grape Strike*. Introduction by Ilan Stavans. Berkeley: University of California Press, 2007.

Espín, Orlando O. *The Wiley/Blackwell Companion to Latino/a Theology.* Chichester, UK: John Wiley and Sons, 2015.

Fernández-Armesto, Felipe. *Our America: A Hispanic History of the United States.* New York: W. W. Norton, 2014.

González, Erualdo R. *Latino City: Urban Planning, Politics, and the Grassroots.* New York: Routledge, 2017.

González, Juan. *Harvest of Empire: A History of Latinos in the United States.* New York: Penguin, 2011.

Gordon, Diana R. *Village of Immigrants: Latinos in an Emerging America.* New Brunswick, NJ: Rutgers University Press, 2015.

Gutiérrez, Ramón A, with Tomás Almaguer, eds. *The New Latino Studies Reader: A Twenty-first-century Perspective.* Berkeley: University of California Press, 2016.

Hayes-Bautista, David E. *La Nueva California: Latinos from Pioneers to Post-millennials.* 2nd edition. Berkeley: University of California Press, 2017.

Jaksić, Iván, ed. *Debating Race, Ethnicity, and Latino Identity: Jorge J. E. Gracia and His Critics.* New York: Columbia University Press, 2015.

Matthiesen, Peter. *Sal Si Puedes: Cesar Chavez and the New American Revolution.* Introduction by Ilan Stavans. Berkeley: University of California Press, 2000.

Niccetelli, Susana, with Ofelia Schute, and Otavio Bueno, eds. *A Blackwell Companion to Latin American Philosophy.* Malden, MA: Wiley-Blackwell, 2009.

Pawel, Miriam. *The Crusades of Cesar Chavez: A Biography.* New York: Bloomsbury, 2014.

Soyer, Michaela. *A Dream Denied: Incarceration, Recidivism, and Young Minority Men in America.* Berkeley: University of California Press, 2016.

Stavans, Ilan. *The Hispanic Condition: The Power of the People.* Revised edition. New York: Harper, 2007.

———, ed. *Latin Music: Musicians, Genres, Themes.* Westport, CT: ABC-Clio/Greenwood, 2014.

———, ed. *The Norton Anthology of Latino Literature.* New York: Norton, 2011.

———. *On Borrowed Words: A Memoir of Language.* New York: Penguin, 2002.

———. *Spanglish: The Making of a New American Language.* New York: Harper, 2003.

Stavans, Ilan, with Frederick Aldama. ¡*Muy Pop! Conversations on Latino Popular Culture*. Ann Arbor: University of Michigan Press, 2013.

Stavans, Ilan, with Jorge J. E. Gracia. *Thirteen Ways of Looking at Latino Art*. Durham, NC: Duke University Press, 2014.

Stavans, Ilan, with Iván Jaksić. *What Is la Hispanidad?* Austin: University of Texas Press, 2011.

\_\_\_\_\_, ed. *Latin Music: Musicians, Genres, Themes*. Westport, Connecticut: ABC-Clio/Greenwood, 2014.

\_\_\_\_\_, ed. *The Norton Anthology of Latino Literature*. New York: Norton, 2011.

# INDEX

*187 Reasons Mexicanos Can't Cross the Border* (Herrera), 138

Academia Norteamericana de la Lengua Española, 159
Aceves, José, 123
Acosta, Oscar Zeta, 126, 138, 139
Adams, John, 14
Agosín, Marjorie, 112
Agricultural Labor Relations Act of 1975 (California Legislature), 57
Agricultural Workers Organizing Committee, 53
Al-Qaeda, 81
*Alamo, The* (film), 23
Alamo (San Antonio, Tex.), 22, 23, 174
Alarcón, Francisco X., 99
Alberto Torres, Carlos, 146
Alcaraz, Lalo, 124
Alfau, Felipe, 135, 136
Algarín, Miguel, 137
Alianza Federal de las Mercedes, 54
Alinsky, Saul David, 48
Allende, Isabel, 139
Allende Gossens, Salvador, 75
Alurista, 137
Alvarez, Julia, 71, 72, 136
*Always Running* (Rodriguez), 96
*America is in the Heart* (Bulosan), 53
American Broadcasting Co. (ABC), 127, 158
*American Family*, 128
American G. I. Forum, 47
Amherst College, 156
Anaya, Rudolfo, 107, 135, 143
Andrade, Oswald de, 9
*Anna in the Tropics* (Cruz), 126
Anthony, Marc, 66

Anti-Defamation League, 111
Anza, Juan Bautista de, 17
Anzaldúa, Gloria Evangelina, 57, 99, 174
Arau, Sergio, 129
Arena, Bruce, 147
Arenas, Reinaldo, 140
*Ariel* (Rodó), 10, 28
Arista, Mariano, 25
Arnaz, Desi, 127
Arte Público Press, 142
Austin, Stephen F. (Stephen Fuller),'
*Autobiography of a Brown Buffalo, The* (Acosta), 138, 172
*Autobiography of William Carlos Williams* (Williams), 137
Aztecs, 51, 52, 91, 101, 103, 106, 125, 145, 150, 174

Baca, Jimmy Santiago, 143
Baca, Judy, 123
Ball, Lucille, 127
*Ballad of Gregorio Cortez, The* (film), 129
*Bamba, La*, 126, 129
Banderas, Antonio, 130, 175
*Bandido* (Stavans), 139
Barretto, Ray, 120
*Barrio Boy* (Galarza), 157
Basquiat, Jean Michel, 122
Bates, Katherine Lee, 24
Batista y Zaldívar, Fulgencio, 43, 44
Behar, Ruth, 112
Ben, Jorge, 119
Bernstein, Leonard, 96, 174
Betances, Ramón Emeterio, 64
Biberman, Herbert J., 56
Bible, 13, 103–107, 161, 173

*Biblia del Oso* (Pineda), 105
Bilingual Education Act (1968), 154
Bilingual Press/Editorial
    Bilingüe, 142
Billington, James H., 138
Blades, Rubén, 120
*Bless Me, Ultima* (Anaya), 107, 143
Bolívar, Simón, 2
*Border-Crosser with a Lamborghini*
    *Dream* (Herrera), 138
*Borderlands/La Frontera* (Anzaldúa), 99
Borges, Jorge Luis, 135, 139
Bowie, Jim, 23
Bracero Program (1942–1964), 33, 46
Bradford, William, 59
*Brief Wondrous Life of Oscar Wao, The*
    (Díaz), 136
Brooke, John Rutter, 31
*Brown* (Rodriguez), 100
Brown University, 156
Brownell, Herbert, 79
Buarque, Chico, 119
Buena Vista Social Club, 120
Bulosan, Carlos, 53
Burgos, Julia de, 66
Bush, George, 57, 158
Bush, George W., 75, 80, 97, 102,
    158, 167
Bush, Jeb, 167
Bush, Prescott Sheldon, 102

Cabañas González, Roberto, 146
Cabrera, Lydia, 133, 134
Cabrera Infante, Guillermo, 140
California, University of, 57
*Canción de la verdad*
    *sencilla* (Burgos), 66
Cantinflas, 9, 174
Cardozo, Patricia, 129
Caridad del Cobre, Virgen de la, 91,
    107, 108, 173
*Carreta, La* (Marqués), 125
Casas, Bartolomé de las, 88, 156
Castañeda de Nájera, Pedro de, 17
Castellanos, Juan de, 13
Castillo, Ana, 57
Castro, Fidel, 4, 43–46, 67–70, 75, 120,
    133, 154, 172
Castro, Joaquín, 41
Castro, Julián, 41
Castro, Raúl, 45
Catholic Church and Catholicism, 4,
    12, 13, 15, 18, 50, 56, 87, 90, 92,
    93, 98, 101–110, 113, 122, 160, 172
Census Bureau (U.S.), 2, 3, 40, 65, 75,
    81, 94, 111, 174

Cervantes, Lorna Dee, 137
Cervantes Saavedra, Miguel de,
    165, 167
Chacón, Eusebio, 141
Chacón, Filipe N., 141
Chapa, Juan Bautista, 17
Chavez, Cesar, 35, 41, 46–53, 57, 58,
    107, 117, 124, 126
Chávez Frías, Hugo, 75, 76
Cherokee Indians, 159
*Chicano* (Vásquez), 135
*Children of Sánchez, The* (film), 130
*Children of Sánchez, The*, (Lewis), 134
Chinese Exclusion Act (1882), 62, 81
Chong, Thomas, 130
*Chronicle of the Narváez*
    *Expedition* (Núñez Cabeza de
    Vaca), 16
*Chromos* (Alfau), 136
Chumash Revolt (1824), 18
Cienfuegos, Lucky, 137
Cisneros, Sandra, 136
*City of Night* (Rechy), 99
CK, Louis, 174
Clemente, Roberto, 144, 148, 171
Clinton, Bill, 57, 167
Clinton, Hillary Rodham, 38
Cocco De Filippis, Daisy, 72
Collins, Phil, 174
Colón, Jesús, 65
Colón, Willie, 120
Colorado College, 24
Columbia Broadcasting System
    (CBS), 127, 158
Columbia University, 28
Columbus, Christopher, 2, 11, 13, 15,
    70, 134, 160, 166, 173
Congressional Hispanic Caucus, 42
*Corán, El* (Cortés Soroa), 112, 174
*Corán, El noble* (Navío), 112
*Corán, El Sagrado* (Abboud and
    Castellanos), 112
*Corán Sagrado, El* (Hallak), 112
Coronado, Francisco Vásquez
    de, 17, 21
Corpi, Lucha, 171
Cortázar, Julio, 139
Cortés, Hernán, 102, 106, 145, 160
Cortés Soroa, Julio, 112
Cortez, Gregorio, 117, 129, 133, 172
*Coser y cantar* (Prida), 126
*Cosmic Race* (Vasconcelos), 89
Council of Mexican-American
    Affairs, 41
*Country for All, A* (Ramos), 128
Crespí, Juan, 17

Crockett, Davy, 23
*Cross and a Star, A* (Agosín), 112
*Cross and the Pear Tree,*
    *The* (Perera), 112
*Crossover Dreams,* 129
Cruz, Celia, 115, 120, 173
Cruz, Nilo, 126
Cruz, Ted, 37
Cuban American National
    Foundation, 40, 43
*Cuentos Negros de Cuba* (Cabrera), 134
Customs and Border Protection
    (U.S.), 118

D'Amato, Alfonse, 98
D'Rivera, Paquito, 121, 173
*Diario, la prensa, El* (New York), 135,
    147, 160
DACA (Deferred Action for
    Childhood Arrivals), 177–80
Daly Archive Press, 136
Darío, Rubén, 9, 28
*Darling* (Rodriguez), 100
Davidovsky, Mario, 116
Davis, Miles, 121
*Day Without Mexicans, A,* 192
*Days of Obligation* (Rodriguez), 100
*Death in the Afternoon*
    (Hemingway), 149
*Death of Rubén Salazar*
    (Romero), 132
Deferred Action for Childhood
    Arrivals (DACA), 177–80
Democratic Party (U.S.), 3, 36, 37
Díaz, José, 33
Díaz, Junot, 136
Díaz, Porfirio, 63, 109
Díaz Ayala, Cristóbal, 119
Dickens, Charles, 168
Domingo, Plácido, 116
Dominicans Don't Play (gang), 95
*Don Quixote* (Quixote), 167, 168, 173
Dorfman, Ariel, 112, 143
*Down These Mean*
    *Streets* (Thomas), 66, 87
DREAM (Development, Relief, and
    Education for Alien Minors) Act
    (2001), 79, 80, 171, 177
Dreamers, 177–80
*Dreaming in Cuban* (García), 136
*Drown* (Díaz), 136
Du Bois, W. E. B. (William Edward
    Burghardt), xxvii
Dukakis, Michael S., 159
Durán, Diego, 146
Durbin, Richard J., 79

*Edad de oro* (Martí), 29
Eire, Carlos M. N., 138
Eisenhower, Dwight D., 45, 79
*El Gallo: La Voz de la Justicia,* 55
*El Monte* (Cabrera), 133
*El Norte* (film), 129
*El Paso Herald-Post,* 131
*El Super* (film), 129
*Eminent Maricones* (Manrique), 99
Enriquillo, 156
Equal Employment Opportunity
    Commission (EEOC), 55
Escalante, Jaime, 157, 173
Escobedo, Alonso Gregorio de, 16
*Espejo-The Mirror* (Romano), 142
Estefan, Gloria, 9
Esteves, Sandra María, 137
Estrada Palma, Tomás, 31

*Facundo: or, Civilization and*
    *Barbarism* (Sarmiento), 68
*Family Installments* (Rivera), 66, 87
Fear and Loathing in Las Vegas
    (Thompson), 139
*Fefu and Her Friends* (Fornés), 125
Ferdinand V, King of Spain, 15, 160
Fernández, Mary Joe, 148
Ferré, Luis Alberto, 32
*Fiddler on the Roof,* 127
Figueroa, Sotero, 64, 141
*Florida del Inca, La* (Vega), 17
Font, Pedro, 17
Foraker Act (1900), 31
Ford, John, 23
Foreign Assistance Act (1961), 45
Fornés, María Irene, 125
Fox News, 129, 147
Francis, Pope (1936), 46
Frente Sandinista de Liberación
    Nacional, 73, 74
Fresno Bulldogs (gang), 95
Fricke, Charles Williams, 33
Friedan, Betty, 56
From the Other Side of Night
    (Alarcón), 99
Fuentes, Carlos, 139

Gadsden, James, 26
Gadsden Purchase (1854), 1, 21, 26,
    52, 82, 89, 104, 157
Galarza, Ernesto, 157
Gallo, El, 55
Gandhi, Mahatma, 46, 48
Garcés, Francisco Tomás
    Hermenegildo, 17
García, Chino, 66

García, Cristina, 136
García, Frank, 122
García Márquez, Gabriel, 139
García, Orlando Jacinto, 116
Garza, Carmen Lomas, 175
*George López Show, The*, 114, 128
*Gift of Time, The* (Ramos), 128
Gil, Gilberto, 119
Gillespie, Dizzy, 121
Ginsberg, Allen, 137
Ginsburg, Ruth Bader, 42
Goliad Massacre (1836), 22
Golijov, Osvaldo, 116
Gómez, Máximo, 29
Gómez-Peña, Guillermo, 126
Gonzáles, Rodolfo (Corky), 41,
    46, 54, 55
González, Elián, 70
González, Ricardo (Pancho), 148
González, Xavier, 123
Grant, Ulysses S. (Ulysses Simpson), 71
*Great Expectations* (Dickens), 168
Guadalupe, Our Lady of, 9, 49, 90,
    105, 106, 107, 172
Guadalupe, Victoria Yolí Raymond
    (La Lupe), 120
Guadalupe Hidalgo, Treaty of (1848),
    1, 7, 21, 25, 26, 27, 35, 47, 49, 52,
    54, 58, 60, 82, 89, 95, 104, 124,
    134, 141, 157
Guerra, Juan Luis, 119
Guevara, Che, 44, 45, 46, 49, 139,
    156, 171
Gutiérrez, Frank, 72

Hackford, Taylor, 96
*Half of the World in
    Light* (Herrera), 138
*Hamilton*, 127
*Hamlet* (Shakespeare), 168
*Hammon and the Beans,
    The* (Paredes), 134
Hanna-Barbera Productions, Inc., 124
Harvard University, 156, 157
Hatch, Orrin, 79
Hayakawa, S. I. (Samuel Ichiyé), 163
Hayworth, Rita, 130
*Heading South, Looking
    North* (Dorfman), 112
Hearst, William Randolph, 28
Heine, Heinrich, 143
Hemingway, Ernest, 149
Henríquez Ureña, Camila, 157
Henríquez Ureña, Max, 157
Henríquez Ureña, Pedro, 72, 77,
    156, 157

Hernández, Ester, 175
Hernandez, Gilbert, 124
Hernandez, Jaime, 124
Herrera, Juan Felipe, 138
Hidalgo y Costilla, Miguel, 21, 105
Hijar y Jaro, Juan Buatista, 141
*Hijo de la tempestad, El* (Chacón), 141
Hijuelos, Oscar, 136
Hinojosa, Maria, 131
Hinojosa, Rolando, 135
*Hispanic Condition, The* (Stavans), 102
*Historia de la Nueva Mexico* (Villagrá),
    17, 134
*Historia del Nuevo Reino de León de
    1650 a 1690* (Chapa), 17
*History of Texas, 1673–1779* (Morfi), 17
Holman, Bob, 137
Hostos, Eugenio María de, 64, 141
*House on Mango Street,
    The* (Cisneros), 136
Houston, Sam, 22, 23, 172
Houston, University of, 142
*How the Garcia Girls Lost Their
    Accent* (Alvarez), 136
*How the Other Half Lives* (Riis), 66
Huerta, Dolores, 35, 41, 46, 56, 57, 124
*Hunger of Memory* (Rodriguez), 99
Hussein, Saddam, 76, 81

*I am Joaquín* (Gonzáles), 55
*I Love Lucy*, 114, 127, 172
Ichaso, León, 129
*In the American Grain* (Williams), 137
*In the Heights*, 127, 171
*In the Time of the
    Butterflies* (Alvarez), 71
Insfrán, Julio César Romero, 146
Immigration Act (1917), 32, 83
Immigration and Nationality Act
    (1952), 81, 83
Immigration and Nationality Act
    (1965), 84
Immigration and Naturalization
    Service (U.S.), 79
Immigration Reform and Control Act
    (1986), 80
Inquisition, 103, 104, 110, 174
*Interviews/Entrevistas*
    (Anzaldúa), 99
Iran-Contra Affair, 74
Iroquois Indians, 159
Irving, Washington, 134
Isabella I, Queen of Spain, 15, 160
Islam, 4, 15, 103, 111, 112
Island Called Home, An (Behar), 112
*It Calls You Back* (Rodriguez), 96

Jackson, Jesse, 41
Jefferson, Thomas, 14
Jesus Christ, 90, 92, 103, 104, 106, 109
Jiménez, José (Cha-Cha), 41, 52
Jobim, Antonio Carlos, 78
John Paul II, Pope, 18, 108
Johnson, Lyndon B. (Lyndon
    Baines), 39, 54
Jones, William Atkinson, 63
Jones-Shafroth Act (1917), 1, 32,
    63, 173
Juana Inés de la Cruz, Sister, 56,
    156, 174
Judaism, 4, 15, 103

Kagan, Elena, 42
Kahlo, Frida, 49, 102, 109
Kennedy, John F., 45, 54, 117
Kerry, John, 158
King, Martin Luther, Jr., 46, 48, 52
Kino, Eusebio Francisco, 13, 15, 141
Klinsmann, Jürgen, 147
Knight of Elvas, 16
Kreutzberger Blumenfeld, Mario
    Luis, 129
Kubitschek, Juscelino, 78

Labyrinth of Solitude, The
    (Paz), 102
Latin American Literary Review
    Press, 143
Latino Wave, The (Ramos), 128
Lau v. Nichols Trail (1974), 162
Laviera, Tato, 137
Lazarus, Emma, 61
League of United Latin American
    Citizens, 47
Legend of la Llorona, The (Anaya),
    98, 143
Lewis, Oscar, 134
Light in the Dark/Luz en lo
    Oscuro (Anzaldúa), 99
Literary Currents in Hispanic
    America, 157
Little Prince, The (Saint-Exupéry), 168
Locos (Alfau), 135
Logan Heights Gang, 95
Lopez, George, 114, 128
Lopez, Jennifer, 118, 131
López, Yolanda, 124
Lorenz, Ricardo, 116
Los Angeles Daily News, 33
Los Angeles Herald-Express, 33
Los Angeles Times, 33, 131, 172
Love and Rockets (Hernandez), 124
Lowry, Malcolm, 109

Maceo, Antonio, 29
Machado y Morales, Gerardo, 43, 44
Maduro, Nicolás, 76
Maine (Battleship), 29
Major League Soccer, 146
Making Face/Making
    Soul (Anzaldúa), 99
Malinche, 91, 102
Mambo Kings Play Songs of Love,
    The (Hijuelos), 136
Man of La Mancha, 167, 173
Manifest Destiny, 19, 20, 24, 28
Manrique, Jaime, 99
Many Deaths of Danny Rosales,
    The (Morton), 126
Marcos, Subcomandante, 149, 156
Mariel Boatlift (1980), 69
Marín, Francisco, 64
Marín,, Roger Anthony (Cheech), 130
Marinho Chagas, 146
Marquéz, René, 125
Martí, José, 64
Mary Magdalene, Saint, 106, 107, 109
Mas Canosa, Jorge, 41
Mayas, 73, 145, 159, 162
McCain, John, 38
McKinley, William, 30, 31
Mencia, Carlos, 114, 128
Menéndez, Ramón, 129
mestizaje, mestizos, and mestizas, xxvii,
    3, 7, 9, 12, 16, 46, 52, 73, 89, 90,
    91, 99, 107, 108, 123, 161
Mexican-American Political
    Association, 43
Mexican-American War
    (1846–1848), 7, 14, 24, 25, 26, 27, 82
Mi querida Isabel, 128
Miami Vice, 128
Miller, Yvette E., 143
Mind of Mencia, 128
Minnesota, University of, 156
Miñoso, Orestes, 148
Miranda, Carmen, 78, 119, 130, 174
Miranda, Lin-Manuel, 127, 171
Monroe, James, 24
Monroe Doctrine, 24, 30
Montezuma II, Emperor of
    Mexico, 27
Moraga, Cherríe, 57
Morfi, Juan Agustín, 17
Morton, Carlos, 126
MS-13 (gang), 95
MSNBC, 129
Muñoz Marín, Luis, 32
My Beloved World (Sotomayor), 42
My Mexican Shivah (Stavans), 110

Nabokov, Vladimir
    Vladimirovich, 135
*Narrative of the Coronado
    Expedition* (Castañeda de
    Nájera), 17
Narváez, Pánfilo de, 16, 161
Nascimento, Mílton, 119
National Association of Latino
    Elected and Appointed
    Officials, 42
National Broadcasting Company
    (NBC), 127, 158
National Chicano Liberation Youth
    Conference, 55
National Chicano Moratorium
    Committee, 132
National Council of La Raza, 42
National Farm Workers
    Association, 53, 57
National Gang Center, 96
National Puerto Rican Coalition, 42
Nava, Gregory, 129
Navajo Indians, 21, 159
Nebrija, Antonio de, 160, 174
Ñetas (gang), 95
*New York Journal-American*, 28
*New York World*, 28
Nieto-Gómez, Anna, 20
Nixon, Richard M. (Richard
    Milhous), 2, 174
Niza, Marcos de, 13, 17
North American Soccer League, 146
North Carolina, University of, 112
Northside Bolen Parque 13 (gang), 95
*Nuevo Herald, El* (Miami), 147, 160
Núñez Cabeza de Vaca, Alvar, 13, 16,
    21, 173

Obama, Barack, xxix, 38, 41, 45,
    46, 80, 97, 177
Obejas, Achy, 99
*Obituario puertorriqueño* (Pietri), 66
O'Farrill, Chico, 121
Olmos, Edward James, 96, 126
Olmecs, 145
*On Borrowed Words* (Stavans), 110, 113
Oñate, Juan de, 13, 17
Operation Bootstrap, 65
Opinión, La (Los Angeles), 147, 160
*One Hundred Years of Solitude* (García
    Márquez), 139
Operation Peter Pan (1960–1962), 69
Operation Wetback (1954), 79
Orozco, José Clemente, 123, 124
Ortega, Daniel, 74

Ortega y Gasset, José, 28
Ortíz, David, 148
*Other Face of America,
    The* (Ramos), 128
O'Toole, Peter, 173
*Oxford English Dictionary* (OED), 59

*Pa'lante*, 53
Pacheco, Johnny, 120
Padilla, Heberto, 140
Palmieri, Charlie, 120
Palmieri, Eddie, 120
Palóu, Francisco, 17
Paredes, Américo, 133, 134
Paris, Treaty of 1898, 31, 64
Parker, Charlie, 121
Partido Revolucionario
    Institucional, 149
Paz, Octavio, 140
*Pearl, The* (Steinbeck), 16
Peña Nieto, Enrique, 20
Perera, Victor Haim, 112
Pérez, Danilo, 121
Peter, the Venerable, 112
Pierce, Franklin, 26
Pietri, Pedro, 66
Pineda, Juan de, 105
Piñero, Miguel, 125, 137
Pinochet Ugarte, Augusto, 74
Pirandello, Luigi, 135
*Pirates, Indians and
    Spaniards* (Escebedo), 17
Pizarro, Francisco, 161
Platt Amendment (1901), 31, 44
Playboys (gang), 95
*Pocho* (Villarreal), 135
*Poems, Protest, and a Dream* (Juana
    Inés de la Cruz), 174
Political Association of
    Spanish-Speaking
    Organizations, 43
Polk, James K., 24, 25
Pomona12th Street Sharkies
    (gang), 95
Portinari, Cândido, 78
Posada, José Guadalupe, 102
Prescott, William Hickling, 134
Prida, Dolores, 126
Protestantism, 4, 109
Pueblo Indians, 21
Pueblo Revolt (1680), 18
Puente, Tito, 66, 115, 120
*Puerto Rican in New York, and Other
    Sketches* (Colón), 65
Pulitzer, Joseph, 28

Querétaro Protocol (1848), 26
*Qur'an*, 144, 172, 174

Ramirez, Manny, 148
Ramírez, Martín, 122
Ramos, Jorge, 128
Ramos, Manuel, 139
Ranjel, Rodrigo, 16
Raya, Marcos, 123
*Raza, La* (Chicago), 147, 160
Raza Unida Party (U.S.), 55
Reagan, Ronald, 43, 74
Real Academia Española, 159
*Real Women Have Curves*, 129
Rechy, John, 99
Reno, Janet, 70
*República Deportiva*, 147
Republican Party (U.S.), 3, 37, 43
*Resurrection Boulevard*, 128
*Revolt of the Cockroach People,
   The* (Acosta), 138
Revueltas, Rosaura, 56
Ribera, José Rómulo, 141
Richardson, Bill, 167
Riis, Jacob A. (Jacob August), 66
Rincón, Bernice, 56
Ríos Montt, Efraín, 73
Rivas, Bittman (Bimbo), 66, 137
Rivera, Chita, 130
Rivera, Diego, 102
Rivera, Edward, 123
Rivera, Tomás, 135, 142
Rodó, José Enrique, 10, 28
Rodriguez, Luis J., 96, 143
Rodriguez, Richard, 99, 100
Rodriguez, Robert Xavier, 130
Rodríguez de Tió, Lola, 64, 141
Romano-V., Octavio Ignacio, 142
Romero, Frank, 132
Romney, Mitt, 38
Roosevelt, Theodore, 30, 172
Rosas, Juan Manuel de, 68
Ross, Fred, 48, 57
Roybal, Edward R., 41
Roybal-Allard, Lucille, 41
Rubalcaba, Gonzalo, 121
Rubio, Marco, 37
Ruiz Belvis, Segundo, 64
Ruíz de Burton, María Amparo,
   135, 172

*Sábado Gigante*, 129
Saint-Exupéry, Antoine de, 172
Salazar, Rubén, 126, 131, 132
*Salt of the Earth*, 56

San Jacinto, Battle of (1836), 22, 23
Sánchez, Alfonso, 54
Sánchez, Chalino, 118
Sandino, Augusto César, 73
Santa Anna, Antonio López de,
   22, 23, 25
Santayana, George, 143
Santería, 9, 108, 113, 134
Santos, Daniel, 120
Sarmiento, Domingo Faustino, 68
Schifrin, Lalo, 116
Seguín, Juan Nepomuceno, 41
Segura, Pancho, 148
Selena, 117, 118, 130
Serra, Junípero, Saint, 17, 18
Serrano, Andrés, 98, 99
Sessions, Jeff, 179
Shakespeare, William, 28, 67, 135, 168
Shakira, 115
*Short Account of the Destruction of the
   Indies, A* (Casas), 88
*Short Eyes* (Piñero), 125
*Shrunken Head of Pancho Villa,
   The* (Valdez), 126
*Simplemente María*, 128
Siqueiros, David Alfaro, 123, 124
Sleepy Lagoon Case (1942), 32, 33, 34,
   35, 138, 172
Slim, Carlos, 111
Smithsonian Institution, 26, 29, 132
Somoza Debayle, Anastasio, 73
Somoza Debayle, Luis, 73
Somoza García, Anastasio, 73
Sondheim, Stephen, 96
Sonora Matancera, La, 120
Sosa, Omar, 121
Soto, Gary, 137
Soto, Hernando de, 16
Sotomayor, Sonia, 42, 173
*Spanglish* (Stavans), 165
Spanish-American War (1898), 4, 19,
   27, 28, 29, 30, 31, 63, 66, 94, 108,
   110, 117
Spanish Civil War (1936–1939),
   135, 136
*Spy Kids*, 130
*Squatter and the Don, The* (Ruíz de
   Burton), 135, 172
*Stand and Deliver*, 157
Steinbeck, John, 16
Steinem, Gloria, 56
Stockton College (San Joaquin Delta
   Community College), 57
Suarez, Ray, 131
Sureños (gang), 95

Taylor, Zachary, 25
Telemundo, 127, 128, 146, 158, 160
Teller Amendment (1898), 31
*Tempest, The* (Shakespeare), 28, 67
Texas, University of, 131, 133
*This Is How You Lose Her* (Díaz), 136
*This Bridge Called My Back* (Anzaldúa and Moraga), 99
Thomas, Piri, 66, 87, 138
Thompson, Hunter S., 138, 139
Thoms, William John, 133
*Tigres del Norte, Los*, 118
Tijerina, Reies, 35, 41, 46, 53
Toltecs, 145
Torres, Luis A., 141
Torres-Saillant, Silvio, 72
Travis, William Barret, 23
*True Relation of the Vicissitudes That Attended the Governor Don Hernando de Soto* (Elvas), 16
Trujillo Molina, Rafael Leónidas, 71
Trump, Donald, xxiii, xxiv, xxv, xxix, 20, 38, 43, 45, 80, 84, 89, 97, 129, 159, 178, 179
*Two Rode Together*, 23

Unamuno, Miguel de, 28
*Uncle Remus con Chile* (Paredes), 134
*Under the Volcano* (Lowry), 109
United Farm Workers, 46, 48, 49, 51, 53, 57, 94, 107, 126, 132, 171
Univision, 127, 128, 129, 146, 147, 158, 160
Urrea, Luis Alberto, 143

Valdés, Bebo, 121
Valdés, Chucho, 121
Valdés, Germán (Tin-Tan), 9, 172
Valdés, Zoé, 140
Valdez, Luis, 102, 125, 126, 129, 130, 173
Valens, Ritchie, 126
Valenzuela, Fernando, 174
*Vanguardia, La*, 168
Vargas, Getúlio, 77
Varrio Nuevo Estrada (gang), 95
Vasconcelos, José, 52, 89, 99

Vassar College, 157
Vásquez, Richard, 135
Vega, Bernardo, 65
Vega, Garcilaso de la, 16
Veloso, Caetano, 119
Vergara, Sofia, 174
*Versos sencillos* (Martí), 29
Vigil, José María, 141
Villa, Pancho, 102, 105, 126, 174
Villagrá, Gaspar Pérez de, 17, 134
Villaraigosa, Antonio Ramón, 167
Villarreal, José Antonio, 135
Virgil Pichardo, Osvaldo José, 148
*Viva Zapata!*, 130
Voting Rights Act (1965), 37, 38

Walt Disney Corporation, 124
Washington, George, 14, 175
Wayne, John, 23
*We came all the way from Cuba so you could dress like this?* (Obejas), 99
West Side Story, 96, 130, 174
White Fence (gang), 95
Wiesel, Elie, 41, 60
Williams, William Carlos, 137
Williams College, 156
Wilson, Tom, 132
*With His Pistol in His Hand* (Paredes), 133
Whitman, Walt, xxiii
*Who Would Have Thought It?* (Ruíz de Burton), 135

xenophobia, 180

*Y no se lo tragó la tierra* (Rivera), 142
Yale University, 102, 156
Yáñez, René, 123
Young, Robert M., 129
Young Lords, 41, 52, 55, 132, 172

Zangwill, Israel, 6
Zapata, Emiliano, 105, 139
Zapotec Indians, 145, 162
*Zoot Suit* (Valdez), 102, 126, 129
Zoot Suit Riots (1943), 32, 34, 35, 138
Zumárraga, Juan de, 106